DEATH INVESTIGATION

ABOUT THE AUTHOR

Lieutenant Terry L. Castleman retired from the Sangamon County Sheriff's Department, Springfield, Illinois with 25 years of experience, and 20 of those years were as a death investigator. He has a degree in Law Enforcement Administration and has completed numerous courses offered by the prestigious Department of Pathology, St. Louis University School of Medicine in St. Louis, Missouri. An instructor and lecturer, he has presented classes and lectures to thousands of police officers, prosecutors, coroners, and pathologists across the country. He has consulted on several homicide cases throughout the United States.

He is a past member of the Illinois Police Association, the Michigan Society of Forensic and Investigative Hypnosis, the International Society of Forensic and Investigative Hypnosis, the Midwest Homicide Investigators Association, the American Society of Law Enforcement Trainers, the Illinois Coroners and Medical Examiners Association and past President and member of the Fraternal Order of Police. Lt. Castleman currently holds an active membership with the International Association of Bloodstain Pattern Analysts.

DEATH INVESTIGATION

A Handbook for Police Officers

By

TERRY L. CASTLEMAN

Lieutenant, Retired
Sangamon County Sheriff's Department
Springfield, Illinois

Charles C Thomas
PUBLISHER • LTD.
SPRINGFIELD • ILLINOIS • U.S.A.

Published and Distributed Throughout the World by

CHARLES C THOMAS • PUBLISHER, LTD.
2600 South First Street
Springfield, Illinois 62794-9265

©*2000 by* CHARLES C THOMAS • PUBLISHER, LTD.

ISBN 0-398-07104-7 (hard)
ISBN 0-398-07105-5 (paper)

Library of Congress Catalog Card Number: 00-042304

With THOMAS BOOKS *careful attention is given to all details of manufacturing
and design. It is the Publisher's desire to present books that are satisfactory as to their
physical qualities and artistic possibilities and appropriate for their particular use.*
THOMAS BOOKS *will be true to those laws of quality that assure a good name
and good will.*

Printed in the United States of America
CR-R-3

Library of Congress Cataloging-in-Publication Data

Castleman, Terry L.
    Death Investigation : a handbook for police officers / by Terry L.
Castleman.
        p. cm.
    Includes index.
    ISBN 0-398-07104-7 (laminated) -- ISBN 0-398-07105-5 (pbk.)
    1. Homicide investigation. I. Title.

HV8079.H6 C37 2000
363.25'9523--dc21
                                                              00-042304

The thousands of investigative hours conducted by the men and women deputy sheriffs of the Sangamon County Sheriff's Department in central Illinois during the homicide of our friend and fellow police officer, Deputy Sheriff William D. Simmons, must be noted. Their professionalism and perseverance through nearly two painful decades before the killer was convicted must also be recognized. I know that the murder of Deputy Bill Simmons touched the hearts and lives of all who called the Sangamon County Sheriff's Department home. With this in mind, this book is dedicated to the men and women, past and present, who proudly wear the uniform of the Sangamon County Sheriff's Department.

CONTRIBUTORS

THE LATE GRANT C. JOHNSON, M.D.

Memorial Medical Center
Department of Pathology
Springfield, Illinois

LT. JOHN LEWIS (RETIRED)

Sangamon County Sheriff's Department
Springfield, Illinois

PREFACE

THIS HANDBOOK IS INTENDED to be an investigative resource for all police officers who are charged with the responsibility of investigating death. It is written to be both an in-depth and quick reference guide. It will help the development of the necessary skills that any police officer utilizes during the course of each death investigation.

Drawing upon two decades of experience as a police death investigator and 15 years of teaching death investigation-related courses to thousands of police officers, prosecutors, emergency medical personnel, coroners and pathologists, the various aspects of cause and manner of death are examined in this book

This manual has been written to provide relevant educational material for persons who will be involved in the scientific or legal circumstances relating to the investigation of death. The book defines the role of the police death investigator, discusses numerous manners of death, defines procedures for investigating the crime scene, techniques for identification of the unidentified victim, methods for proper handling and transport of the body, and establishes methodical approaches to any death investigation. Pertinent information relating to the basic understanding and use of innovative investigative techniques such as the use of hypnosis, bloodspatter interpretation and psychics are examined.

The police officers that will be involved with death investigation need to develop and enhance his or her own style of approach to this type of investigation.

This handbook is suitable for the college law enforcement or criminal justice student, and may be also utilized as a supplemental study guide for death investigation-related college courses.

T.L.C.

INTRODUCTION

I SPENT TWENTY-FIVE YEARS as a Sangamon County (Springfield, Illinois) Deputy Sheriff. It was the most rewarding career that anyone could ever hope to achieve. In the 20 years that I spent working death investigations, I had the distinct honor of having solved more than 50 consecutive murders. Although all murders were important to me, there was none more meaningful than solving the seventeen-year-old murder of my friend and fellow officer, Deputy William D. Simmons.

I cannot tell you how many deaths that I actually investigated during this time, as there were simply too many. I can say that I attended more than 300 autopsies. Once I even assisted in the performance of a postmortem examination. It had to be one of the strangest things that a police officer can ever do. If I could ever live my life over, I would be a forensic pathologist.

For years other police officers asked me to teach them how I did what I did when it came to death investigation. I hesitated in doing so because I did not know why I was successful investigating deaths. I dismissed it saying, "What works for me may not work for you." This attitude changed shortly after attending a Bloodspatter Workshop in Minnesota, instructed by Bart Epstein and Terry Labor. I learned a great deal from the information they taught. However, it was not until I returned home and attempted to share what I had learned with some pathologists from Memorial Medical Center that I truly understood what I had learned.

From that point on, I began teaching classes. I taught at Lincoln Land Community College, The Springfield Police Academy, The Illinois State Police Academy and with the local mobile training unit. I taught classes in: death investigation, bloodspatter interpretation, crime scene investigation, crime scene processing, interview and interrogation techniques, and forensic hypnosis. These were classes that I had attended and I did not realize my own knowledge and expertise in these areas until I began to share what I had learned. It seemed that the more I taught and shared with others, the more I learned. I have now shared my knowledge with more than 3,000 medical examiners, coroners, lawyers and police officers from five different states.

I would like to point out one important factor that cannot be learned simply by reading this book, or any book, and cannot be taught in a classroom. For any investigation to be successful you must have TEAMWORK. Sangamon County law enforcement went through a very painful growth in homicide investigation that lasted nearly a decade. It is paramount that every person in a death investigation know the significance of teamwork. This includes all law enforcement, prosecutors, coroners, medical examiners, and crime laboratory personnel.

I don't know why teamwork was such a problem. No one seemed to work together, and everyone thought that everything was someone else's job. Well-known news commentator Paul Harvey was once given credit for saying, "If you want to get away with murder, do it in Sangamon County." That was pretty much true for the time period from 1960 through 1970. About this time, J. William Roberts, became the states attorney. He stated, "We will all work together. We will suffer the burdens together, and we will rejoice in our triumphs." This philosophy was long overdue, and it worked.

This handbook contains information that can be used for in-depth reading about specific information, or for quick reference. This information is intended to assist you with various types of death investigation. I hope that you will find this book not only interesting, but helpful in conducting any investigation you are involved with. It is with knowledge and experience that we can perform all the necessary tasks which must be done in all death investigations.

It is with utmost importance that I embrace the memory of the late Dr. Grant C. Johnson, forensic pathologist. I have truly only admired two men in my life. One was my late father, for having taught me about life. The other was Dr. Johnson, for having taught me so much about death. All that I was, as a death investigator, I learned from the teachings of these two men. Dr. Johnson treated me like a son and he spent countless hours teaching me about life after death and the forensic evidence that a corpse can provide. The days of examining the hundreds of victims of death, and the endless nights of rolling on Dr. Johnson's living room floor role-playing a victim's last moments alive, shall forever be remembered.

ACKNOWLEDGMENTS

It saddens me that I cannot acknowledge by name everyone that had a positive influence on me during my career in law enforcement.

There are several people that must be noted, for without them, this book would not have been written. I must mention the late Grant C. Johnson M.D., and all the medical staff of the Department of Pathology, Memorial Medical Center, Springfield, Illinois. Thank you for having patience with me, and sharing your expertise in the investigation of death.

To J. William Roberts, former Sangamon County States Attorney, Springfield, Illinois and Justice Benjamin K. Miller, Illinois Supreme Court; I thank you for providing your legal knowledge and experiences.

I must also make mention of six of my friends and co-workers that had a positive impact on my investigative career. From the Sangamon County Sheriff's Department, Springfield, Illinois, Chief Loren Larsen (Retired), Captain John Pyle (Retired), Lieutenant Jack Lewis (Retired), and Sergeant Rick Miller: your confidence, continual support, and the invaluable assistance that made our department so successful with so many homicide investigations.

To Professor Ivan Wright, Lincoln Land Community College, Springfield, Illinois. It was through your efforts that I began teaching. Thanks for all your help at the college.

To Commander Marcia A. Lange (Retired), Springfield Police Department, Springfield, Illinois, I started my investigative career with you and will end it with you. Thanks for all your support.

A heartfelt acknowledgment and thank you to my wife, Laurel J. Castleman. Your support in my teachings and writings has meant so much to me. You are such an important part in my life and in all that I have become.

To my mother, Fairy Castleman, thank you for all your help. Mom was such a good listener and she heard about all my cases. She also told me at the beginning of my police career to write things down and put it in a book someday. Well, mom, here it is.

To Mrs. Pat Pemberton, Bachelors in Journalism, who helped perfect this manuscript, thank you for your countless hours on this endeavor.

To Mr. Michael Payne Thomas, publisher, without his sharing of knowledge and expertise, this handbook could not have been completed.

CONTENTS

DEATH INVESTIGATION

Try to understand that all my life I have believed that all things happen for a reason. We may not know why at first, but eventually we will understand all that happens. I have also concluded that we will learn from these things in our lives that do happen. Life is given to us to live as we choose, but it is taken away from us by death. This happens all too often without offering any choices at all.

Terry L. Castleman

Chapter 1

DEATH DEFINED

THE OLD ADAGE that only two things are certain, death and taxes, is fairly accurate. Some folks may not pay taxes, but the single most absolute fact in life is that everyone will die. Biologically speaking, the course of death is an eventuality. Different tissues and organs in a living body die at different rates. We can break down death into two categories.

Molecular Death: Different tissues die at different intervals. The brain may die but the muscles respond to electrical stimulation for several hours.

Clinical Death: Death as a whole, failure of the body, respiration and circulation cease.

SUDDEN UNEXPECTED DEATH

Definitions

Sudden: Quick or not expected.
Unexpected: Usually refers to death occurring in a healthy person. Sudden unexpected deaths are related to natural causes (see Chapter 15 for Sudden Infant Death). Some 60 percent to 70 percent of all deaths that come under the jurisdiction of the coroner or medical examiner are due to natural causes. The establishment of cause of death in sudden or unexpected deaths calls for good investigation. Beware of one manner of death masquerading as another. Listed below are two examples of events that can produce a natural death.

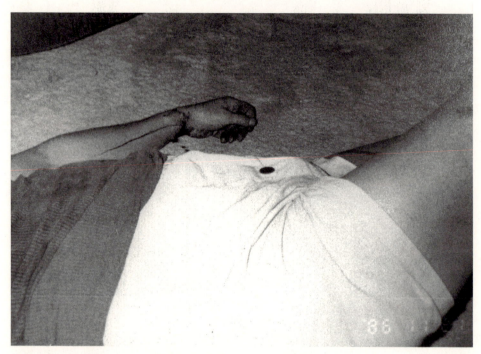

Figure 1.1. One form of death can masquerade as another form. Initial observation would indicate that the victim may have died as a result of suicide. Very little blood was found. The victim actually died from pneumonia.

Natural Causes of Death

Heart Attack: (Number one killer)
Symptoms:
1. Shortness of breath
2. Pains in chest

Stroke:
1. Clot in brain area
2. Cerebral hemorrhage
3. Embolism–air in circulatory system

Symptoms:
1. Paralysis on side of body
2. Dizzy
3. Difficulty of speech
4. Affects memory

The autopsy reveals the most probable cause of death; it may not necessarily be incompatible with life but there is no other reason or explanation. A competent investigation may avert the need for an autopsy. However, if there is any doubt, then have an autopsy performed. It would not be unusual for the family to request an autopsy. Family members will want to know the reason that their loved one died.

Legal concerns of actual death must be considered. In some instances persons are kept alive by artificial means. Should the life support be removed the victim may or may not die. However, in the matter of harvesting organs, the victim must be kept on life support to insure that the transplants of such organs as the lungs, liver or heart are feasible.

Depending on your personal, ethnic or religious opinions, you may hold many different beliefs about death. Some people consider as true that when you die, that is the end. The body simply turns to dust. Others believe that after you die you are reincarnated, into someone or something else. Other beliefs are that when you die you go to be judged for the deeds of your life on earth. At this point you are cast into Purgatory, condemned to Hell or rewarded with Heaven. Still there are some that are of the opinion there is a place or a horizon that is in between life and death. Life after death, without our own beliefs, how do we know what is and what is not true. You will need to have your own thoughts and feelings about what happens after you die. You will also need to honor and respect the beliefs of others.

Chapter 2

THE ROLE OF THE DEATH INVESTIGATOR

PERHAPS BECAUSE I COME from the old school, I have always believed that hands-on experience is always the best way to learn about death investigations. There are two very significant problems with this thought. First, it is not possible to learn if not given the opportunity to do so. Second, in a major case it is not always possible to share knowledge and expertise with so much riding on an investigation. From the arrival of the first officer on the scene, everything that is done and in some cases not done, becomes extremely crucial.

The coroner, or the coroner's physician, or the medical examiner is responsible for the body. Law enforcement is responsible for the scene. The body is a part of the scene, therefore the death investigator must be satisfied that everything that can be done, has been done prior to any moving or removal of the body. In jurisdictions across the country the medical examiner or the coroner has the legal responsibility of investigating all violent, suspicious or sudden deaths. It is therefore necessary that the death investigator knows who is responsible for all types of death, within his or her jurisdiction. It is imperative that the investigator knows what can and cannot be done. Neither the coroner nor the pathologist is going to conduct the investigation into how this death occurred, or in some instances, who caused the death, that is the responsibility of the police. Remember, any successful endeavor involving more than one person requires total cooperation.

There are several categories of death that should be investigated by the death investigator. All violent deaths, non-violent deaths of persons under the age of 40, all suspicious deaths, deaths at the workplace and deaths that occur while in custody. There are five types of death that the police need to be concerned with: homicide, suicide, accident, natural and unknown. One might ask why a natural death should be

6

of concern to the police. The reason for this is because any type of death can be disguised as another type.

Because of the vast amount of authority that the police death investigator has, your integrity must never be compromised. It is not unusual to be approached by others in your department, police officers from other agencies or prominent political or social figures who will attempt to influence you or your findings in a particular case. Police officers must be prepared to investigate the many circumstances of all forms of death. They can only do this effectively if they have reached a high level of competency. This competency can only be attained by having the desire and interest in this type of work, the necessary knowledge and training, and, of course, experience. A good death investigator is a good listener. The death investigator must listen to what people have to say. You must also be able to explain any information that has been developed. You must also possess compassion. Treat all people with consideration and respect. The death investigator has to have a great deal of patience, persistence and a positive attitude. These types of cases take time to investigate, some take years or even decades. Lastly, one cannot work in this gruesome vocation and expect to endure without a good sense of humor.

It is important that the death investigator have a plan of investigation. Although not all cases are the same, we can still preplan and be prepared. It is so critical that all police officers involved in a death scene know, understand, and follow their roles. This preplanning should include a strategy of approach, into the scene not only for the safety of the officers responding, but for the preservation of pertinent evidence. The protection of life is the most significant aspect of any type of police response. Once the scene is entered and secured, numerous photos should be taken immediately. These Polaroid™ pictures should be retained by the death investigator and used to assist the pathologist with the performance of the postmortem examination. The Polaroid photos provide the pathologist with an opportunity to observe the body's position and location when it was first discovered.

One major function of police at the scene is to gather and record the facts of the investigation. There are two equally important methods of gathering the facts. The first one is by observance, while the second is to listen to what is reported to you by other officers or witnesses. Be absolutely positive you fully understand what is told to you. It is far better to ask a question a second time and get the same answer, than to accept as fact information that is not fully understood. At that point you must accurately record this information.

The death investigator should then review the scene. Look for the obvious observations first. Things such as apparent injuries that may give any immediate indication as to what caused the death. All observations made at the scene should be recorded immediately. This can be accomplished with the use of rough notes or utilization of a tape recording device. The death investigator should be attentive to even the smallest of details that seem like they would not matter in the long run. Upon completion of the review of the scene, 35 mm photographs and a video or videos should be made. After all photographs and videos have been made, then a closer on-scene examination of the victim should be completed.

The review process actually begins again with the complete review of the body. You should look for injuries or wounds. Look for items such as: scratches, broken fingernails, bite marks, blood, bruises, semen or gun powder. Describe in complete detail all observations. After all observations pertaining to the examinations of the body have been recorded, Polaroid photos of the victim displaying those observations should now be taken. Finally, 35 mm stills and videos of the deceased can be completed.

At this point, accurate measurements should be taken. The use of a chalk outline around the body can also be performed. The purpose of these measurements is so that the body can be removed from the scene, and yet for all intent and purpose it could be placed back exactly where it was located. After all measurements are taken, bag the hands and the feet by placing separate paper sacks over each hand and foot. These sacks should be secured in place with tape. This preserves any evidence that may be located there such as soil, blood, hair or skin.

The body is now ready for transport to the morgue. The coroner may check the body for identification and remove such items as a driver's license. If the pathologist is on scene he or she might examine the victim by removing items of clothing; however, there is no reason for any other item to be removed from the body. The body should then be wrapped in a white sheet and placed into a body bag and sealed. Note that nowhere in this chapter has it been written to place a cover over the body. Important evidence has been lost or contaminated by placing a blanket on a victim and then taking the blanket off for examination. The body, accompanied by a police officer for chain of custody purposes, should be transported directly to the morgue by a designated ambulance or coroner's vehicle. The police officer will then sign the body into the morgue.

Once the body has been removed from the scene, the collection of physical evidence can commence. In some agencies the death investigator may be charged with the responsibility of collecting evidence. Whether the death investigator is required to collect evidence or not, has no significant impact on the investigation. However, it is paramount that the death investigator has a complete understanding of all facets of the evidence related to a death investigation. The value of evidence and how it relates to the investigation often proves or disproves the type of death that may seem apparent.

Now that all observations from the scene have been recorded, preliminary examination of the body completed and photographs taken, and all the evidence having been collected, it is time for the death investigator to put his or her experience to work by analyzing the facts. The police investigator must focus on what type of death can be proved, the identity of the victim and the identity of the offender, if there is one. If an offender is suspected, the death investigator must also consider the motivation for the death and the progression of events leading up to the death.

It is suggested that whenever possible the police death investigator witness the autopsy of the deceased. Very valuable information can be ascertained from the findings of the pathologist. You should meet with the pathologist prior to the postmortem examination of the victim. Be prepared to answer any questions that might be asked of you concerning the investigation. It is important that the death investigator take the Polaroid pictures to the autopsy for the pathologist to review. Any other instruments that may have been used to facilitate the death, such as a gun or knife, should also be taken to the autopsy for the pathologist to review or compare to any findings. It is up to the death investigator to familiarize the pathologist with pertinent facts from the scene.

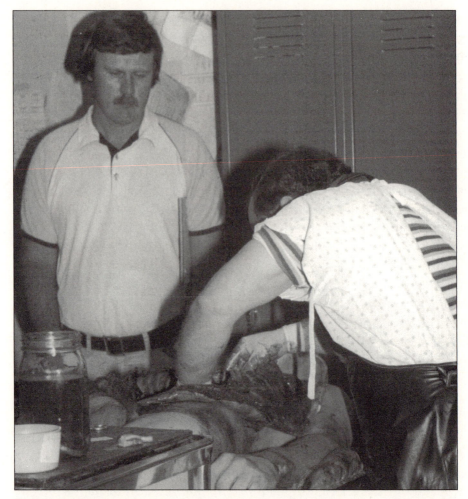

Figure 2.1. A function of the police death investigator is to attend the autopsy of all death cases that are to be investigated. Not only to provide pertinent information to the pathologist but also to learn more concerning how or why the victim died.

The autopsy examination however gory, is the victim's way of giving up information about how life was taken. When attending the autopsy, you must realize that this is a time to learn more about how death was brought about, or how or why it occurred. Forensic autopsies differ greatly from a general autopsy. In a general autopsy, the pathologist will look mostly for the cause of death whereas the forensic autopsy will not only be looking for cause but also the manner of death, as well as any other factors which might be involved. Unfortunately, forensic autopsies or postmortem examinations will vary from one hospital to another, depending on the protocol of a specific hospital. Other information that should be provided to the pathologist, is the environmental temperature at the death scene and other pertinent data such as whether lights were on or off, if mail or newspapers were present, etc. Information should also be provided concerning environmental conditions such as weather, temperature, moisture, humidity and conditions surrounding the victim at the scene.

An important and yet difficult aspect that can fall under the role of death investigator, is that of death notification to the next of kin. Not all police officers are capable of responding to this situation. The death investigator must be ready for a variety of responses from the victim's family. People who are given notice that a loved one is deceased will react differently. Some people will drop to the floor or chair, while others will become combative and strike out at the individual bringing this devastating news. Some relatives will not want to view the victim, while others will wish to spend some final moments with their loved one. In many instances, valuable information can be learned during this initial contact. Family members may be less likely to discuss the victim or the victim's activity as time goes on. You must be sensitive, but you must also establish pertinent facts about the victim.

The police death investigator may be called upon to testify at a coroner's inquest or other legal proceedings. You must be prepared, should you be required to give testimony concerning the facts surrounding a death. Preparation can be in the form of reviewing all reports pertinent to the case. Be truthful and confident in your testimony. Your courtroom demeanor is also very important. Conduct yourself in a polite, courteous and professional manner. Give equal responses to both the prosecutor and the defense attorney. Do not let an attorney get you upset, keep emotions under control. Do not provide more of an answer than the question requires. If you do not know the answer to a question, say so. Coroners and prosecutors enjoy putting a well-prepared witness on the stand to present the facts of the case.

Lastly, the role of the police death investigator is to make the case. Determine the proper manner of death and seek an arrest and conviction in those cases where death was at the hands of someone else. **REMEMBER,** never compromise yourself or your investigation. Always conduct a death investigation right the first time, you may never get a second chance. The police death investigator is the only representative that the deceased shall ever have. It is the responsibility of every police officer that investigates death to assist in training new investigative personnel. You must keep up-to-date on new investigative tools and techniques. A death investigator must maintain an objective approach while conducting methodical and systematic investigations.

DEALING WITH THE MEDIA

As a police death investigator, it may become necessary for you to deal with the media. You should cooperate as much as possible to create a win-win scenario. The media will consider it a win if they can obtain a story. You can win by providing selected information to the public. You need to be honest, brief and positive. It will also help to practice dealing with the media.

It is important to be prepared and know what you are going to say. Sometimes what you want to say and what you do say is not always the same. Often the media will approach you before you have had the time to get prepared. It is at a time like this that you need to excuse yourself for a few minutes and get prepared. You can say you have an important page to answer that may be related to the investigation, or you need to use the restroom. The media will wait for you, be assured.

When addressing the media, do not get angry or upset. Always conduct your media interviews on the highest professional level. You do not want to act overly friendly to the reporters, however, you do want to be courteous and respectful. Always return reporters telephone calls, even if it is late in your day. Do not make any comments that are considered "off the record." Your comment or remarks can appear in the news.

You should provide only facts that can be released. Keep press statements or answers brief. Do not give incomplete information. If only pieces of certain information can be released, then do not give out any of that particular information. Remember that it is not only possible to say too little, it is just as possible to say too much. Do not make your answers too vague, it will only call for additional questions by the media.

Most police death investigators consider it breaking a cardinal rule to leak or provide unauthorized information to the media.

Unfortunately, this type of unprofessional behavior has happened in the past and it will happen again in the future. The leaking of pertinent information about a death investigation can only hurt the investigation. This information can be leaked by other death investigators, other police officers, prosecutor's and the victim's family members.

Keep good eye contact with the media. Release only information that can be released; information that will not place the investigation in jeopardy. Avoid comments such as, "I don't know" or "No comment." Develop an organized pattern of news releases that is given each time that you address the media. It may be helpful to have your own recording of the news conference to be absolutely positive what information you did release.

CASE FILE REVIEW

It is the responsibility of the death investigator to insure that the complete case file has been put together and properly organized. This includes:

Police Reports

1. Initial call to police.
2. Initial police reports.
3. Follow-up reports.
4. Evidence reports or log sheets.
5. Photographs, slides, video and audiotapes.
6. Crime laboratory reports.
7. Notes, sketches, graphs and charts.

Autopsy Reports

1. Copy of morgue logbook.
2. Autopsy findings, protocol.
3. Photographs, slides, graphs and charts.
4. Reports of evidence recovery and transmittal for chain of custody.

Coroner's Reports

1. Inquest records, testimony and depositions.
2. Death certificate.

List of Names

1. All police personnel.
2. All medical, fire and emergency personnel.
3. All pathology personnel.
4. All crime laboratory personnel.
5. All coroner's office personnel.
6. All secretarial personnel that type reports.

Chapter 3

IDENTIFYING THE VICTIM

PERHAPS ONE OF THE MOST significant duties of the police death investigator is to establish the identity of the victim. Identification is the recognition of an individual as determined by characteristics, which differentiate that individual from all others. Identification is necessary so that a legal certification of death can be made. Furthermore, identification of the remains provides the corpus delicti for all subsequent legal actions. Once an identity is determined, additional leads for information can be developed. Information such as the victim's family or friends, or perhaps the victim's employment records or finances will provide additional leads. A check for romantic involvement or criminal records can be initiated.

Many times the victim can be visually recognized because the physical features have not been distorted by death or injury. In some situations the body can be visually identifiable for a short period of time. Within thirty minutes the body may no longer be recognizable due to postmortem changes. When a body is discovered you must make a thorough and accurate description immediately. Use your Polaroid® as soon as possible.

Methods used to establish identity are dictated by the postmortem conditions of the body. Discoloration of the skin and bloating of the body caused by gaseous decomposition may make the natural likeness distorted. Mutilation of the deceased may occur in several ways. Animals, aquatic life, boat propellers, fire or heat, explosions, trains, automobiles or other large moving vehicles can cause mutilation. An assailant, to hinder identification attempts, may deliberately mutilate the body. All of these forms of mutilation can make visual identification difficult if not impossible.

Bodies recovered from fires present extremely difficult problems in identification. Several artifacts can be noted in identification of the burned body. Bodies can lose several inches in height and 60 percent of body weight, giving a totally different appearance to the victim. Head hair can be burned off or hair color can change.

A complete description of unidentifiable bodies should include the following: approximate age, sex, race, height, weight, complexion, eye color and hair color. Additional summary of the face, ears, teeth, limbs, scars, marks and tattoos should be noted. Also include descriptive information about clothing, keys, jewelry, eyeglasses or hearing aids. Keep in mind that fingerprint and dental records may not always be available for use in identification.

Figure 3.1. Positive identification of all victims is crucial. This subject was found in the passenger seat of a vehicle that had been set on fire. Identification is this type of death can be extremely difficult.

Law enforcement officers should be aware of the numerous problems with the unknown dead. Such bodies may be in a non-decomposed state, in a state of decomposition but with no bones exposed, semi-skeletal remains with very little flesh present, or totally skeletal without flesh. Likewise, the wearing apparel and other personal property found at the scene may be in varying conditions from new or undamaged to decayed beyond ordinary recognition. It is not unusual that bodies are mistakenly identified as a friend or relative by well-meaning but emotionally distraught people. For this reason the identification of the corpse is a very serious problem for the police death investigator. It is your responsibility to establish accurate identification of the body by the physical remains and other evidence in cooperation with the coroner, medical examiner or pathologist.

Identification Categories

1. Bodies that are not decomposed or mutilated, and can be identified visually.
2. Bodies that cannot normally be identified by visual means:
    a. decomposed bodies (wet or dry floaters).
    b. bodies burned beyond recognition.
    c. bodies that are mutilated or damaged beyond recognition.
    d. bodies that have been skeletonized by animal activity or through decomposition.
    e. bodies that have been cremated.

Features Used in Identification

1. Complete description of the entire body, weight, height, tattoos, scars and deformities.
2. X-rays, old injuries, abnormalities of bones, bullets and other foreign matter.
3. Complete dental evaluation.
4. Complete blood grouping, typing and DNA.
5. Fingerprinting, palm prints and footprints.
6. Complete skeletal examination. Useful in determining sex, race, age and stature, usually lacks positive identification data.

7. Hair studies.
8. Smears of cells for sex identification.
9. Careful examination of personal effects.
10. Various foreign objects in the body, wire structures, pacemakers or prostheses.
11. Distinctive disease process.
12. Identification by circumstance.

Identification Procedures

1. Photograph facial features. If identification cannot be established, the following procedures need to be completed.
2. Obtain finger and palm prints, and footprints.
3. Obtain full dental examination.
4. Have full body x-rays taken.
5. Note any injury, or surgical scars.
6. Note any deformities, or amputations.
7. Note any birthmarks.
8. Note any warts, moles, or tumors.
9. Note any tattoos.
10. If body is skeletonized, determine sex, race, approximate age and individual characteristics.

Chapter 4

CAUSE AND MANNER OF DEATH

I THINK THAT THE FIRST ITEM that needs to be addressed is just what is death? When you are dead, are you dead? Today doctors, lawyers and judges argue over at just what point you are dead. In early times, death occurred when you stopped breathing. Now questions arise about life support systems and the use of the term *brain dead.* Whenever I am discussing the finer points of being dead, I recall the phrase Dr. Grant C. Johnson had used so frequently, "Obviously and Irrevocably Dead."

The police death investigator has three procedures at hand to assist in making a determination if life is present. Any of the three can be utilized. Perhaps the simplest method is to check for a breath. This can be done by observing the victim's chest. Look closely for a few moments, any breathing can be observed by the rising and falling of the chest and abdomen area. If this cannot be observed, then the victim is not breathing or breathing is very shallow. Shallow breathing can be very difficult to detect. Remember, that lack of breath does not indicate that the victim is positively dead.

The second technique that can be employed to determine if life is present, is checking for a pulse. You can check the pulse by using the tips of your fingers. Your fingers can be placed on the inside of the wrist, or along either side of the neck or throat. If the victim has a heartbeat, then a pulse can be felt. No pulse would indicate that death has occurred, it certainly is indicative that the person is not breathing.

The third observation that can be accomplished is to check the eyes and the changes in the pupils. Since the eyes are extremely sensitive tissues, if life is present some activity in the eye should be noted. Death will cause the eyes to dry out and lose muscle control. If the eyes are open at the time of death, they will not close. The shine in the eyes will be gone. The pupils will no longer respond to light.

It has often been said that police officers do not have to make the determination if someone is deceased. However, more than once in my career I have had to make that determination. When I arrived on a scene where the person was obviously irrevocably dead, I still requested the coroner and paramedics. Every police officer needs to fully understand that at some point in his or her career they will get a call to respond to a victim possibly deceased. More times than not, a police officer will be the first person on the scene. You will have to make the call.

I recall when I first started teaching death investigation classes to police officers. I would ask how many officers would touch a dead body. Usually more than half would say that they would not. It is important that when you arrive and the area is safe, you need to check the body. Check the body for a pulse, and to see if the body is warm or cool to the touch. The lack of pulse would give some indication that the person might just be deceased. The warm or cool touch could be an indication of how long the individual has been dead. Depending on your department procedures, it would most likely be best to request paramedics or EMT to check the victim for any vital signs of life.

The final word on the time of death is the responsibility of the medical examiner, or the coroner. Even though they may never show up at the scene, it is ultimately up to their respective offices to set the time of death. Often the time of death is set at the time the body was discovered. Any movement or removal of the body should only be done under the direction of the M.E. or the coroner. As stated earlier, an important part of the investigation is teamwork. As a police officer you may have the least say-so at a death scene. However, if you or your department are going to be responsible for the investigation into how this person died, then you need to be satisfied with what has been done at the scene before you allow the body to be removed. Once anything in the scene has been altered, you cannot put it back without some possibility of error. Be sure you have everything you need. The statement that the body belongs to the coroner and the scene belongs to the police is only partially correct. A more accurate statement, would include the phrase, "The body is in the crime scene and therefore is a part of the crime scene."

As soon as death occurs, changes in the body begin to take place.

These changes do not happen all at once. There is some time relationship between death and the changes that will come to pass. Not always do we know the precise time of death. These changes can assist us in determining a range of time that death could have occurred. Time of death is one of the most crucial elements in any death investigation. However, as you will learn there are no hard rules in determining an accurate time that death took place. There are two terms that are important for a death investigator to understand before we delve into the actual investigation of the dead. The terms "Cause of Death" and "Manner of Death" are synonymous with death investigation; however, they hold two totally separate meanings.

Cause of Death

The cause of death is defined as a disease or injury, which directly or indirectly brought about death, brief or prolonged.

Manner of Death

The manner of death is defined as a legal matter that requires an expression or opinion of a medical examiner or a corner's jury. Fashion in which cause of death occurred; homicide, suicide, accident, natural or undetermined.

Mechanism of Death

A physiologic derangement or biochemical derangement produced by cause of death which is incompatible with life.

The police death investigator should focus on the manner of death. Determining cause of death; the disease or injury which directly or indirectly brought about death, is the responsibility of the medical examiner or the coroner. There are five types of death that may be considered as the manner of death that police officers should be concerned with, natural, accident, suicide, homicide and undetermined. It is the job of the death investigator to help prove or disprove which manner of death is related to each victim by determining what caused the death. It is imperative that the death investigator realize that any manner of death can masquerade as another. This especially holds true when neither the cause nor manner can be determined. Death can take place under certain circumstances that give false indications as to the manner of death. It would be extremely difficult to prove a murder that never happened.

It is pretty much the standard now, that all investigations are worked down and not up. What this means is a death investigation should be worked as a homicide until homicide can be ruled out. The case should then be investigated as a suicide until suicide can be disproved. Lastly, work the case as an accident and from there as a natural.

Never work an investigation from natural to a homicide, too much evidence may be lost. **REMEMBER,** any manner of death can masquerade as another form. The police death investigators may find themselves in an impossible situation trying to determine the actual cause of death if the correct manner is not determined. It is sad to say that if mistakes are made in a death investigation, people who commit murder may never be held accountable for their horrible deeds. You are now the only representative the victim will ever have.

Chapter 5

ESTABLISHING TIME OF DEATH

I T IS PARAMOUNT THAT THE closest time of death be learned from your death investigation. It will help in determining the sequence of events leading up to and including that time when death occurred. As written earlier, changes in the body after death may be used to help assist in determining the time of death. One key element that all death investigators must always keep in mind, is that due to different environmental conditions there are no hard and fast rules. These changes after death can only provide a basic guideline for death investigators to work with. Usually the time of death is just an estimate on the basis of the interval between the times that the individual was last known to be alive and when the body was first found. Although the exact time of death may not be precisely pinpointed, at least a range of time that death occurred might be established.

BODY TEMPERATURE

In a living being the metabolism of the tissues generates heat which is very tightly regulated by the body to a narrow range. After death this heat production ceases and the body cools to the approximate ambient temperature. Normal body temperature is 98.6 degrees F. Normally there is a one-hour lag period immediately following death where the body temperature remains fairly stable. After one hour, the body temperature will cool at about one and one-half degrees per hour. However, the body temperature is a narrow range, not a fixed temperature. Activity, illness, the decomposition process, infection, drug intoxication (specifically, cocaine), and absorption of heat can maintain or raise body temperature after death. The body cools by radiation, convection, and direct transfer so that any factors that influence heat loss affect the rate. The environment will have an effect on body temperature. Other factors such as the victim's clothing, if the victim was sick or running a higher temperature, will also have an influence in the rate of lost body temperature. The victim's activity prior to death will also affect the rate of body heat loss. If the victim was involved in any form of strenuous activity heat loss will be affected. Careful consideration of the scene, must be considered in interpreting cooling rate. Was the victim located in open air or water? The victim's size and clothing may also affect the cooling rate.

The most reliable temperature readings are obtained from the rectum without interfering with the body. Temperature readings from the liver, after introducing a thermometer through an incision, are also dependable. Unless specifically trained by a medical examiner or by a pathologist, police officers should not take liver temperatures. Liver temperature is approximately 99 degrees F. Oral temperatures are not recommended.

LIVOR MORTIS

Livor mortis is known as lividity. Lividity is caused by dilation of blood vessels, and settling or pooling of blood in these vessels. Lividity can be noted within minutes of death, but can go unnoticed for a couple of hours. Livor mortis can be mobile for a short time; it then passes from the vessels to the tissues. Once the blood enters into the tissues, lividity becomes "fixed." Normal fixation of livor mortis takes about eight to 12 hours. Prior to this fixation period, lividity will move with any movement of the body. Applied thumb pressure will push the blood away if lividity is not fixed. Livor mortis when fixed is permanent. Lividity gives off a purple discoloration, this is due to the blood no longer receiving oxygen. Bodies that have lost a great deal of blood may show little or no sign of livor mortis. Lividity may be a substantial indicator of the position of the body and objects with which it was in contact with. Pressure against an object may partially be responsible for creating a postmortem mark, which could be misinterpreted as a wound. You should always check the body to insure that the lividity is appropriate. An example of inappropriate lividity would be if the victim was lying face down and the lividity was present on the "backside" of the victim.

RIGOR MORTIS

The term rigor mortis interchanges with rigidity. Rigidity is a well-known phenomenon. Rigor mortis is the process whereby the skeletal muscles enter a temporary period of rigidity due to chemical changes after death. Muscle cells work because of a product in the body called lactic acid. The living body can control the lactic acid, the dead body obviously cannot. When death occurs high levels of this lactic acid form in the muscles. In the time just prior to death high metabolic activity such as exercising, aerobics, swimming, or running, leads to higher levels of lactic acid. Higher environmental temperature also leads to a shorter response time. The general rule of the onset of rigor mortis is that it will begin about 20 minutes after death. I have found that the best way for me to remember the changes due to rigidity is the 12-hour rule. Rigidity takes about 12 hours to be complete, will be present for 12 hours, and begins to disappear in another 12 hours. Rigor mortis will be gone in 60 hours. Always remember that rigor mortis is temporary. Rigidity appears to start at the head and work its way down the body; however, rigor mortis actually starts in the shorter muscles in the face first. It then moves to the longer muscles. Rigor mortis develops in the position the body is in. The death investigator should always check the body to see that the rigidity is appropriate. The environment may greatly influence the development of rigor mortis. The onset of rigidity will be delayed in cold temperatures, emaciated individuals, individuals with chronic disease, and those who are grossly obese.

POSTMORTEM DECOMPOSITION

Postmortem (after death) decomposition is greatly affected by environmental conditions. Internal organisms in the intestine become very active and start multiplying and decomposition begins. First the intes-

tine and the blood will be attacked. When gas formation leads to the
ruptures in the body, other organs will be attacked. Organs start
decomposing at different times after death. Due to the destruction of
body tissues by bacteria, usually from the intestinal tract, the body will
alter and change greatly. These changes will be in the appearance of
decay or decomposition. Alterations include the following: skin discoloration, the bloating and swelling of body tissues, blood and other
body fluids purging from the body openings, putrid odor, skin blisters
and scalp and skin slippage.

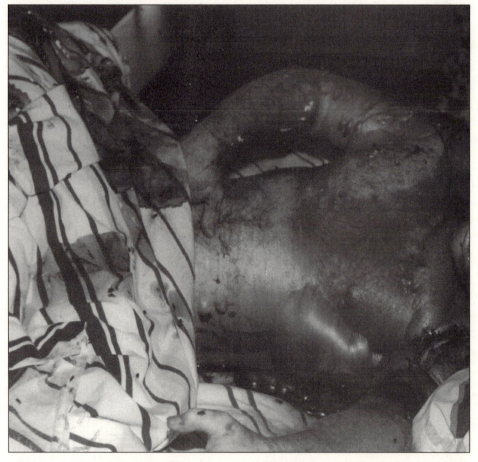

Figure 5.1. This photograph illustrates postmortum changes. Note the discoloration,
bloating and skin slippage.

As mentioned, one obvious change will be indicated by change in color. First evidence of color change is a greenish discoloration in the lower abdomen region. This is followed by a greenish coloration over the entire abdomen. Also observed are interconnecting purplish lines called marbling. Eventually the entire body will have this grayish-green red discoloration. This particular coloration of the decomposed body takes about seven days.

Gas formation tends to begin at roughly the same time as discoloration, usually around 36 hours. The gas formation will produce skin blisters and skin slippage. Generalized swelling of all tissues with protrusion of the eyeballs and tongue occurs. Bloody purging from the mouth and nose can be observed due to rising internal pressures brought about by the gas formation. In about three weeks body cavities will rupture.

LATE POSTMORTEM

Late postmortem decomposition of the body can be divided into several stages, even if the duration of each stage varies considerably. Decomposition is said to be affected by cold and warm temperatures. Cold delays the decomposition while heat increases it. Therefore, the hotter the environment, the quicker the rate of decomposition. Decomposition is thought to develop at a quicker rate if exposed to air than if in water. However, decomposition develops faster in water than in soil. The death investigator should be aware of three types of late postmortem changes. Each is significantly different because they are influenced by different factors.

Three Categories of Postmortem Changes

Putrefication: Caused by bacterial growth in the body. Shows a definite discoloration of the skin. Skin slippage as well as scalp detachment can be observed. The body will also begin to purge fluids from within the body. Bloating that occurs can make the body two to three times its normal size. It would not be unusual to see this late state of decomposition in as little as 12 hours. All of these factors make positive identification extremely difficult.

Mummification: This aspect of decomposition is brought on by lack of moisture. The skin will shrink, giving the false indication that fingernails or hair is still growing. Once all the moisture and fluids are purged the body will dry out and become very leathery.

Adipocere: The body being in water or damp soil brings on this form of decomposition. Again, the rate of decomposition is slower in water or soil than in the open air. As the body decays it takes on a soapy-like appearance. Adipocere can develop in about three months and can remain for several months up to a year.

Case History 1

In one weekend I had two unrelated death investigations where the bodies were found within one mile of one another. It was a Saturday in mid-August when the body of male in his seventies was found in a nearby river. He had been missing for approximately seven months. On Sunday the body of a female in her thirties was found in a cornfield. She had been missing for approximately seven days. Both victims were very similar in late postmortem decomposition. As stated previously, the rate of decomposition is slower in water than in open air. Being in the direct sunlight and the hot summer heat, the female displayed skin slippage and scalp loss, just as the elderly male exhibited having been in the water for seven months.

Case History 2

On a Friday night in July I saw a friend that was a casual acquaintance. On Monday when I was sent to his house, I observed that the house was filled with flies. Upon making my way to the second floor of the home that had no insulation or air conditioning, I observed the same friend that I had seen less that 60 hours ago on Friday. He had one bullet hole to the right temple region. He was bloated to three times his normal size and exhibited skin and scalp slippage. His skin was marbled with green streaks throughout. There was bruising in the face area. I would not have recognized him had I not known that this was his house.

The death investigator needs to be aware that bodies that are exposed to the outdoor elements are subject to postmortem artifacts. Not only will insects feed from a corpse, so will small animals such as foxes, possums, or raccoons. These small animals will eat on the tender portions of flesh. The soft area of the neck is a prime location. This feeding by these animals in the neck area, combined with decomposition, can cause the head and the neck to become detached from the rest of the body. Do not think just because the head is not attached that it is associated with a cutting wound.

FLY LARVAE

After years of removing hundreds of badly decomposed bodies from fields, houses, automobiles and along roadways, I feel that fly larvae should be included in this chapter. In most cases, an entomologist who studies flies, maggots and beetles can, with a significant amount of information collected from a scene, provide the most accurate time of death, as compared with any other factor of postmortem changes. It is with this in mind, that fly larvae is considered in determining time of death. Although a little repulsive, we must keep in mind that maggots are a death investigator's friend. Blowflies will lay eggs in various body openings such as the lips, eyelids, nose, mouth, and in other exposed body orifices just after death or even a short time before death. These fly eggs will then hatch into maggots within about 24 hours. The maggots then feed from the corpse. Since fly activity changes with cooler temperatures and rainfall, these things must be noted if a submission to the entomologist is anticipated.

Due to the various stages of growth referred to as instars, it is imperative that the death investigator collects a sample of all larvae that can be located. The ideal sample would include the oldest to the youngest. It is also necessary to collect the pupa. This pupa resembles rat-like droppings. It is important to understand these stages.

Figure 5.2. The victim has been fully enveloped by maggots. The maggots were used to assist in determination of time of death. The maggots can be very useful.

Stages

1. The blow fly lays the eggs.
2. The eggs hatch into maggots.
3. Maggot encloses itself in a hard brown shell, called pupa.
4. Fully grown flies hatch from the pupa.

Maggots have also been used to do toxicology on a body when no other fluids were available for testing. The maggots are collected and placed into a blender and liquefied. This liquid can then be screened by toxicology. Certainly, in the case of these maggots "you are what you eat." It would certainly be beneficial to have a contact entomologist. The entomologist can provide information to you on how to collect and preserve specimens to be submitted for examination. The entomologist will need several samples, some fresh and others stopped at their current life cycle. Ask the entomologist how he or she wants them collected, both alive and dead. The entomologist will also need to know about previous weather conditions covering the suspected time of death.

Entomology is certainly one area from which any death investigator could learn a great deal of important and useful information. Develop an entomologist contact before the need arises. The entomologist can provide you with the complete history of forensic entomology. The entomologist can also assist you with the recognition of the types of insects that might be found in your geographic area and which species you may need to collect. There are numerous species of flies; however, only a certain variety need to be collected. Likewise, there are many categories of beetle, some are significant and others are not. The entomologist can inform you on how to collect, what to collect, how many to collect. The entomologist will need some fresh and some preserved collections and will direct you as to how to prepare the collection for transport and where to send them.

Information that you will need to provide to the entomologist will be the temperature at the scene and the time at which temperature was taken. The date and time insect specimens were collected (fresh and preserved). The temperature of the body between the time of removal from the scene and the collection of the specimens. The entomologist will also need information that relates to the range of temperatures for some previous determinate amount of time (two weeks).

Case History 1

In studies that I have conducted, these maggots appear to go into a feeding frenzy. During this feeding frenzy, higher air and soil temperatures were recorded close to the body. The maggots generated heat which would accelerate decomposition. Since maggots can jump and climb trees, a check of the immediate area should be done for sample collections. In observing tests conducted with dead pigs, whose viscera is similar to a human, a blanket was used to cover one pig. The maggots in their feeding frenzy appeared to move the blanket from the pig to expose the flesh.

Case History 2

A deceased male infested with maggots was brought to Memorial Medical Center for autopsy. The man was covered by the maggots to such a degree that you were able to make out his arms and face only by searching the body's outline of the feeding maggots.

Time-of-Death Aspects

The only accurate method of determining the time of death is to be there when it happens, and even then you have a small range of error. There is currently no singular accurate marker of time of death. The closer to the actual time of death, the more accurate is the opinion that can be determined from the scene and markers of death. The experience and caution of the police death investigator combined with the classic markers and a well-established window of death, can lead to a possible range of death. To determine the probable range of death, first establish a window of time that death could have occurred. Determine when was the deceased last known to be alive and when was the body was found. The difference is the range of time whereby death could have occurred. Use those scene markers that allow some positioning of the death within the window by the following: mail, newspapers, phone calls, meals eaten, place and state of dress. Adjust the preliminary opinion by additional data that can be gathered about the victim. Consider environmental factors and circumstances that may have changed. Use observations of the degree of rigidity, amount and position of lividity, body temperature, presence of fly eggs or larvae. Use considerable caution on time of death determinations, as there can be factors that markedly enhance or retard the chemistry of death and the body's changes. Don't attempt to make your opinions more accurate that the data allows.

Stages of Postmortem Decomposition

1. Blue green discoloration of the skin (24-36 Hrs.)
2. Marbling, green-black discoloration
3. Bloating   (36-48 Hrs.)
4. Entire body decomposition   (60-72 Hrs.)
5. Skin Slippage   (4 -7 Days)
6. Adipocere
7. Mummification
8. Skeletonization   (Weeks to years)

Environmental Factors

Factors Influencing Postmortem Decomposition
    Temperature
    Humidity
    Location (indoors or outdoors)
    Clothing
    Heat increases rate
    Cold decreases rate
    Insects and soil work from outside in
    Microorganism work from the inside out

Stomach Contents

Stomach empties in 2-6 hours
Small bowel empties in 2-6 hours

Chapter 6

CAUSES OF DEATH

ASPHYXIA (LACK OF AIR)

A BROAD TERM REFERRING to the set of conditions characterized by the interference with the utilization of oxygen. Two specific forms of asphyxia can be demonstrated. The first would be mechanical asphyxia and the second being chemical asphyxia.

HANGING

One form of asphyxia would be hanging. The asphyxia is caused by compression of the neck from the weight of the body. Hanging can be an accident, suicide or homicide. Hanging needs to be investigated fully so that the correct manner of death is determined. It is important that the noose never be untied. The noose should be cut away from the knot. Tie the two ends of the noose together with string, thus preserving the contour of the knot. Hanging occurs if the pressure exerted on the neck is enough to compress the neck structures. It is not necessary for the body to be fully suspended. Loss of consciousness can occur in less than 2 to 3 minutes if the airway is obstructed.

I can't recall if someone told me or if I read it somewhere, but I was always under the impression that it was not unusual for family members to cut down their loved ones and place them in bed. Thus attempting to disguise the hanging as a natural death. I had never seen this particular scenario until one day. I responded to a home where an elderly gentleman was reported to have been found dead in his sleep. It might have been believable except for the large furrow around his neck. The family later admitted to having cut the man down, dressing him in pajamas, and placing him in bed, prior to calling the police.

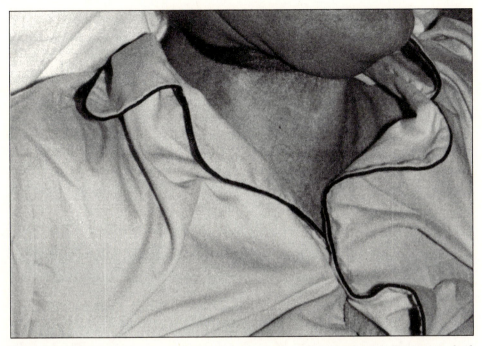

Figure 6.1. The victim was reported to have been found dead of natural causes, in bed and dressed in pajamas. Examination at the scene, revealed a rope furrow around the neck, indicative of hanging.

Ligature marks or furrows can usually be readily recognizable. However, this evidence may be absent if soft or padded material was used. Expect to find similar artifacts and decomposition effects as with ligature strangulation. Also in the face and feet or ankles small pin-like hemorrhages may be seen. These spots are referred to as Tardieu spots. A finding of Tardieu spots is not always indicative of asphyxiation; it can be observed in several other forms of death.

STRANGULATION

As with hanging, strangulation can be an accident, suicide or homicide. This form of asphyxia, is due to the application of force to the neck. Strangulation is broken down into; manual, ligature and yoking. Examination of the neck may provide evidence of the type of the material used or even finger marks. Where lack of air in hanging is the compression of the neck by the weight of the body, strangulation is compression of the neck manually or with the use of a rope or other type of ligature.

Manual Strangulation

Will produce findings such as: nail marks, bruising and internal neck trauma.

Ligature Strangulation

Will produce the imprint of the ligature that may be patterned. This can rapidly disappear during decomposition. Expect to find internal neck trauma.

Yoking

Caused by compression of the neck by using the forearm. Usually will not be able to note trauma to skin. May develop neck bruising in postmortem interval of 12-36 hours.

SUFFOCATION

The prevention of breathing by the blocking of airways is another form of asphyxiation. Sometimes referred to as smothering. Smothering can be accomplished by placing a hand or other object over the nose and mouth. Another form of suffocation would be the use of a plastic bag placed over the head, diminishing the flow of oxygen. The concept of placing a bag over the head is used not only in suffocation, but has also been found in the deaths of persons sniffing glue or other compounds.

In all suffocation cases, especially in infants and the elderly, it is important to check for damage to the frenulum. The frenulum is that cord on the inside of the mouth between the gums and the upper lip that can be felt by the tongue. The frenulum can be damaged during suffocation.

SEXUAL ASPHYXIA

In all these types of asphyxia the possibility of sexual activity must be considered. A sexual perversion called autoerotica occurs when the participant desires to produce a level of cerebral hypoxia by shutting off the intake of air. The premise behind this practice is to heighten sexual satisfaction by going to the point of passing out, then releasing whatever mechanism they are using to restrict the flow of oxygen. This sexual asphyxia, predominately practiced by males between the ages of their early teens to their thirties, is rarely performed by females. Victims of this form of asphyxia may be found fully clothed in their clothing, dressed in women's clothing or totally nude. The presence of sperm is not totally indicative of this type of behavior. Keep in mind that sperm can be present on the male victim of a gunshot wound; therefore, the finding of sperm is not always indicative of sexual asphyxia. It is not unusual to find indication that the victim was attempting or succeeded in masturbating.

The victims of this type of asphyxia will normally be found in an isolated location. Expect to find erotic literature or sexually explicit photographs in the immediate vicinity. Additional scene investigation may reveal evidence that this type of activity has been performed before. Other evidence that the police death investigator should be looking for is an escape mechanism from the ligature or from bondage devices. Evidence of protection to hide activity may also be apparent in the scene.

Autoerotic Fatalities

Autoerotic fatalities are deaths that occur during masturbation. The person may die of natural causes while performing masturbation, or death may be brought on by the use of some type of injurious agent. The euphoric or intoxicating gases that are inhaled during sexual activities can produce death. The manner of death in these types of autoerotic fatalities is asphyxia. These types of deaths can be erroneously thought to be suicide. The euphoric state is created by the use of certain types of gases to replace oxygen. One form of gas that has been widely used is nitrous oxide. There are many gases that can be obtained that will produce a hypoxic state. Another form, fluorocarbon, can be found in aerosol spray cans. It has been determined that fluorocarbons can cause heart attacks when high concentration levels are induced into the body. Chemicals used to enhance the joys of sex are often referred to as aphrodisiacs. Different forms of aphrodisiacs can be found advertised over the Internet and in magazines.

Types

1. Asphyxia, compression of the neck, chest or abdomen
2. Cardiac
3. Toxic agent.
4. Electrocution

Victim Profile

1. Caucasian male 9-30 years of age
2. 40% married
3. Middle class

Implication

1. Manner of death is ***ACCIDENTAL***

CHOKE

Blocking of the internal airway by a foreign object. The object is generally inhaled, but due to its large size it is impacted in the airway. The victim can generally exhale but cannot inhale. Implication as to manner of death is that of accidental.

TRAUMATIC ASPHYXIA

Breathing is hindered by external chest compression by extreme pressure. Scene investigation should establish what happened. This form of asphyxia can be caused by situations such as having a vehicle fall on the chest, or being buried by falling masonry or dirt from a deep trench collapse. Another situation might be from a stampede or by a large crowd pushing forward during a concert or sporting event. In this form of asphyxia look for the head to be filled with blood.

Chapter 7

ASPHYXIA BY POISONING

POISONINGS CAN BE A HOMICIDE, suicide or accident. It is rare to find a homicide as a result of poisoning. Nevertheless, if the police death investigator is to be certain that death was not a homicide from poisoning, it would be reasonable to investigate all poisoning cases as homicide until proven to be caused by suicide or accident. Perhaps homicide by poisoning has become a lost art. The practice of poisoning one's enemies was once thought to be so significant that families of royalty often had servants that had no other responsibility than to be tasters of food.

Determining if a person has died as a result of homicidal poisoning can be one of the most difficult types of homicide to prove. Evidence of poisoning is obtained from having an indication of the symptoms of the victim prior to death. The postmortem examination of the body and the isolation and identification of the poison would be of significant evidentiary value.

Unfortunately, there is hardly any symptom of poisoning which cannot be caused by disease. However, there are conditions of symptoms which provides some indication of poisoning. The onset of certain symptoms and rapid death can be strong evidence of poisoning. Poisons such as arsenic, strychnine, and narcotics can produce similar symptoms as do disease to certain body organs or infections.

In this type of investigation you must gather as much evidence as possible. All substances, foods and drinks should be collected. Determine when the last meal was eaten and if others became sick from eating the same food or drink. Ascertain the state of health of the victim before becoming ill. Find out if the victim has ever tried to commit suicide. The findings of the pathologist and the toxicologist are extremely crucial.

The pathologist will be able understand the effects of certain poisons from the postmortem exam. Acids and alkalis may cause extensive burns around the mouth or surface of the body and do severe damage to tissues. Metallic poisons will cause profound destruction to the intestinal tract, liver, or kidneys. Phosphorus causes a degeneration of the liver. So often in poisoning deaths the pathologist's examination will show that death was not a cause of natural death or traumatic injury. There is no evidence for death other than that of poisoning. Most poisons and drugs do not produce characteristic pathological lesions and can be only established in the body by toxicological analysis. Toxicology is an important avenue in many types of death investigations. In order to obtain a successful prosecution of homicide by poisoning, the police death investigator must be able to establish several factors. The police death investigator must determine or the motive for the crime, the perpetrators, accessibility to poisons, if the assailant was aware of the lethal effects, and if he or she had an opportunity to disperse the poison to the victim. As was indicated murder by poison is certainly not as common as suicide.

Poisons can be classified into several categories by chemical characteristics. One would need to have a strong educational background in chemistry to fully understand the characteristics of all the categories. Included in this chapter are several examples of poisonings that the police death investigator will most likely be asked to investigate. This is one area of death investigation that the death investigator will need to rely heavily on other forensic specialists. Included in this forensic group is pathology, toxicology and chemistry.

Perhaps the most common aspect of poisoning that law enforcement will deal with is death due to carbon monoxide poisoning. As stated earlier in Chapter 6 there are two specific forms of asphyxia. Cited was mechanical and chemical asphyxia. Carbon monoxide, although associated with the chemical form of asphyxia, is a poisoning as far as a cause of death determination. Carbon monoxide as a poison falls into the category of gases. There are numerous gases that are proven to be very poisonous. New gases that are poisonous can be developed by anyone at any time. The big fear during the Gulf War was the manufacture of gases that could be released upon U.S. troops. At the time of this writing the government is still attempting to determine what those troops may have been subjected to during their tour of duty.

CARBON MONOXIDE POISONING (AN ASPHYXIA)

Lack of air in this instance is caused by red corpuscles not being able to carry oxygen to the body's tissues and returning carbon dioxide to the lungs. Carbon monoxide is odorless and colorless. The hemoglobin has an affinity for carbon monoxide 250 times greater than oxygen. Levels of carbon monoxide are determined from the hemoglobin. Fatal levels can be at 40 percent. These fatal levels can be affected by age, young or old, and the use of alcohol or drugs. Death resulting from carbon monoxide poisoning can result within minutes. The body will develop a bright cherry-red color.

The incomplete burning of carbon-based materials causes carbon monoxide. It is found in fires and exhaust from automobiles. Carbon monoxide poisoning can be an accident, suicide or homicide. Although I never had a homicide by carbon monoxide, I investigated several cases that were suicide and an equal number that were accidents. Accidental carbon monoxide poison cases that I investigated always happened in the winter. These accidental carbon monoxide deaths fell within two specific areas. The highest number of deaths being associated with victims who started their vehicle to warm it up without proper ventilation. More than one victim started their vehicles and left them running before opening the garage door. They were found in places such as the house attached to the garage, in the front seat of the car balancing their checkbook, and even with their hands on the overhead door of the garage.

The other area of investigations of carbon monoxide deaths were associated with faulty fireplaces or furnaces. Something as simple as a dirty fireplace flue can cause carbon monoxide poisoning. Ironically, in some instances where there were several people in the house only some were affected by carbon monoxide. Several different investigations indicated that carbon monoxide affects the very young; the elderly; persons with coronary heart disease, respiratory problems, chronic lung disease; and by the use of alcohol or drugs. It was also learned that people who slept further from the fireplaces were less affected.

While investigating suicides by carbon monoxide, I have noted that some people will go to great lengths and resourcefulness to fabricate an apparatus to deliver the carbon monoxide. Some victims created a carbon monoxide delivery system that apparently took a great amount of time to create. All it really takes is starting an internal combustion engine without ventilation.

The carbon monoxide in the blood is reported in terms of hemoglobin saturation. The following are comments relative to the level of carbon monoxide in the blood and body effects:

1. Most normal cases have a carbon monoxide level of less of 5%.
2. Smokers may have up to a 10% or more carbon monoxide in the blood.
3. Levels of 15% may disturb vision and judgment.
4. Levels from 20-30% may be associated with headache and nausea.
5. Levels above 50% are usually fatal.

Case History 1

Receiving a call to respond to a rural location on a cold December day, I arrived to be informed that this was a carbon monoxide-related death. Upon my arrival, I observed a one-vehicle garage separate from the house. In the garage the victim, a 24-year-old male, was lying in the seat of his pickup truck. The vehicle had been running until the gas tank was empty. The victim had a blanket and a pillow. This scenario typically indicated suicide by carbon monoxide poisoning. Additionally, it was learned from the family that the victim had been undergoing some financial problems. The coroner's office was ready to rule the case as suicide. In an interview with the victim's mother, who was positive that her son had not committed suicide, provided information that her son had been getting severe headaches ever since the weather had turned cold. Intrigued by this I returned to the house. Sitting in the house for about an hour I began to suffer a really painful headache. Taking a camera and crawling under the house, I could observe the gas furnace. The pictures that I took revealed that the victim's furnace had a cracked heat exchanger. A local furnace repair man told me that this problem would cause headaches. It was thought that the victim, not being able to withstand the headache, took his blanket and pillow and went to sleep out in his truck. It is also believed that the victim started the truck in the garage to keep warm during the cold December night. There was not an adequate amount of ventilation to remove the carbon monoxide. The coroner's jury ruled the case as an accident.

CARBON DIOXIDE POISONING (AN ASPHYXIA)

The elimination of oxygen is asphyxia. Like carbon monoxide, carbon dioxide is associated to asphyxia; however, as far as the cause of death ruling, it is shown as poisoning. This asphyxia may be caused by a build up of carbon dioxide in a small sealed space. This results in reduction of oxygen by rebreathing. Basically the body takes in oxygen by breathing or inhaling air. The body then releases carbon dioxide by exhaling the used oxygen. When in a closed or sealed area the body is unable to take in oxygen, thus rebreathing the carbon dioxide.

In this situation the carbon dioxide (CO^2) levels rise while the oxygen (O^2) levels decrease. Classic examples of carbon dioxide poisoning cases would be those instances where victims have been found in a closed refrigerator. Scene investigations of this type of death become increasingly important when it is realized that carbon dioxide accumulates after death. It would be significant to make an air collection sample at the scene for analysis for carbon dioxide content.

Carbon dioxide deaths are uncommon for several reasons. Today most laws require doors of refrigerators removed before disposal. Prior to this, small children playing hiding games were frequently found dead of carbon dioxide poisoning. Keep in mind that carbon monoxide is heavier than air. In order for CO^2 to be fatal it must be in high concentrations.

Victims of carbon dioxide experience rapid loss of energy and strength. Therefore they are unable to get themselves out of this environment even though they are aware of the urgency to do so. The scene may give the appearance that the victim could have gotten out if he or she wanted to. This is not the case due to the rapid loss of physical ability; the victim is unable to attempt an escape effort to get free.

Almost any substance when taken into the body in an abundance can produce serious illness or death. However, it is not always the case that a substantial amount of a poisonous substance need be taken to be fatal. Obviously, there are some substances that only a thimble amount of will produce death. Some clues provide very few investigative leads as to the participation of a substance in bringing about death.

Other categories of poison that must be considered by the death investigator are those of chemical compounds, corrosives, metallic or organic compounds. Certainly this is an area where most death investigators will have very little, if any, expertise. Again, it is so important that law enforcement have the highest level of confidence in other forensic specialists. Death by poisoning provides a high degree of difficulty for the death investigator, and he or she must work closely with these forensic experts.

Remember, there are so many different compounds which are lethal if ingested. The toxicologist has a limited amount of material on which to perform an analysis. Therefore, it is important that the death investigator provide the toxicologist with as much information as possible concerning the pertinent facts of the case. This should include any poisons that may be suspected.

Many poisons can be rapidly excreted from the body. In these cases, only very low levels of poison might be detected. Some poisons can be detected for many years, after death. The embalming process and decomposition can severely hamper the toxicologist's ability to determine a poisonous substance.

Chapter 8

DEATHS DUE TO FIRE

DEATH-RELATED FIRES call for the teamwork approach as much as any type of death investigation. Not only is the police death investigator dependent on such individuals as the pathologist, toxicologist or chemist, but now you must work closely with the fire or arson investigator. The death investigator is concerned with cause and manner of death. The fire investigator is just as concerned about the cause and origin of the fire.

There are a good many reasons why fires occur. However, we can divide these reasons for fires into two basic categories. Intentional and accidental fires are fundamental causes of how fires start. Where death is concerned it is imperative for the death investigator to know if the fire was deliberately set or if it was a simple accident. Arson fires can be a big profit for some. Homeowners, car owners, or business owners can attain financial gain, reduce debt or relocate elsewhere. Persons that have other disorders might set fires for other personal or sexual gratification. However, when life is lost due to fires that are set on purpose, the fire can be classified as a homicide. This type of fire might also be used to produce suicide.

The Fire Starter

Malicious

The malicious fire setter most likely suffers from some type of delusion or disorder. These fires are normally directed towards a school, the boss's car, a neighbor's garage or property belonging to a past love relationship.

Unjustifiable

The unjustifiable fire starter will start fires for no reason. This person is most likely a criminal enhancing his chosen career. This type of individual will most likely set fire to a structure after committing a burglary or other theft. Fires may also be started simply to destroy without reason.

Compulsive

A compulsive fire starter will do so after becoming enraged, frustrated or angered due to resentment or jealousy. It would not be unusual for this person to be remorseful after the fact, yet will make every attempt to avoid detection or claim it was an accident.

Impulsive

The impulsive fire starter has a desire to set fires to beautify the neighborhood, or to destroy eye sores or debris. A compulsion justified by the individual that he or she is doing a good deed or even performing a public service.

Hero

The hero is another type of individual to deliberately set fires. This person cannot attain any other form of recognition or fulfillment. He or she will set the fire, make the discovery, and report the fire to the fire department, and even attempt daring rescues. This person hopes to receive recognition or awards.

Intentional

The intentional fire starter could be described as one who uses a fire for sexual gratification. This form of fire is known as pyromania. The fire and the related excitement stimulates the fire starter into sexual fulfillment.

Accidental

The other category for causes of fire is that of accidental. This too can be separated into two subcategories as far as death investigation. One aspect of accidental fire could be due to faulty equipment or electrical wiring, smoking while intoxicated or falling asleep. The unintentional and innocent burning of leaves, trash or other items such as construction debris can spread to adjacent property. Theses types of fires will usually only affect vehicles, houses or other buildings, and dependent on the response of the fire department, damage may be limited.

Children are responsible for a great number of accidental fires. These accidental fires started by juveniles may be as a result of carelessness, playing with matches, other flame sources, smoking, or playing with combustible liquids. Children that become fatality victims of fire may be found in closets or even on top of refrigerators. Do not be surprised by the location of the children that are found by fire fighters.

The death investigator must realize that death can result in these types of fire. Death is not dependent on who started the fire or why it was started. The victim of the fire is still obviously and irrevocably dead. Statistics of fire victims are taking a turn for the better as for rate of survival. With the increase of burn units and their ability to better treat fire victims, more people are being saved. This increase in lives saved in many ways is amazing. Just a few years ago a person with burns over 80 percent of their body, would certainly give way to death.

There are several reasons why people die in fire. The victim can be burned by the fire, flames coming in contact with the body resulting in burning of tissues. The victim dies of smoke inhalation that may or may not contain various toxic gases, or by inhalation of carbon monoxide. Death may result from various traumatic injuries due to structural damage of the building by the fire, blast injuries of the body due to explosions, and injuries due to falls. Others may jump to their death trying to escape the flames.

Other injuries that are related to the fire possibly postmortem, are alterations produced by fire-fighting equipment, such as the effects of an ax or high-pressure hose. Other injuries of this nature could be produced by earth moving equipment or bulldozers during fire excavation. The heat can cause the brain to boil and the skull can fracture, giving an appearance of blunt trauma. In other rare instances death or injury may be caused by the fire causing the discharge of explosives or ammunition.

Certainly one of the most important aspects of the death investigator's task is to determine if life was present prior to the fire. In some instances of murder a fire is started to cover up the crime by destroying evidence. The finding of soot in the nose or airway would be an indication that life was present during the fire. Carbon monoxide in the blood is another indicator of life. The pathology of the burned body will determine precisely if the body was burned before death or after death.

The fire investigator upon completion of the fire investigations will be able to provide pertinent information about the fire. Was the fire a sooty fire? Was the fire extremely hot? This is important information that should be related to the pathologist by the police death investigator.

There are some other factors that could have an influence on fire-related deaths. The very young and the elderly are most affected by the fire. The influence of drugs or alcohol may also be a contributing factor as to why death occurred. Other aspects that may also be taken under consideration are whether disease or injury caused the death. Or was there some evidence that indicated the victim was unable to flee? An obvious example of this would be if the victim was in a wheelchair.

A primary concern in your investigation is to determine who is the burned victim? Identification can be extremely difficult. The fire victim can experience a shortening of the body by several inches caused by the heat drawing up the extremities giving the appearance of the fetal position from heat flexion. The victim can also undergo a weight loss of 60 percent due to loss of the body's water. The soot from the fire can change the appearance greatly and is extremely difficult to remove. Hair loss and change of color will also exceedingly change appearance. Gray hair can turn a brassy color, while brown hair can change to red.

Figure 8.1. The victim died as a result of a house fire. The deceased gave an appearance of being a young black male in his twenties. The victim was actually a caucasian male, in his late seventies.

DEGREES OF BURNING

First Degree:

> Superficial, outer layer only with blisters. Peeling may occur especially as body is handled, suggesting ruptured blisters. If victim survives, no scarring will result.

Second Degree:
> Adds blistering. If victim survives, usually may heal without scarring. Similar to decomposition blisters.

Third Degree:

Damage to full skin thickness. Areas may be painless because nerve endings are damaged. Healing is from edges. Usually skin must be grafted.

Fourth Degree:

Most severe. Charring, loss of skin, subcutaneous tissue or even body parts. Usually suggests postmortem burning in addition to burning during life. Blood can become a red hard brick material.

Estimation of Body Surface

Nine percent of surface each front and each lower extremity, back of each lower extremity (total 36%), front and back of each upper extremity (18%), anterior trunk (18%), posterior (18%), face and neck (4 1/2%), scalp (4/12%). Without special burn treatment those over 50% total second degree (burn) or worse are usually fatal. Today there are some fire victims saved at 80% burned. Severity of burns depends upon the time of exposure and intensity of fire.

The police death investigator should be aware of other facts during this type of investigation. Always leave any clothing, jewelry or any other personal items found on the body exactly where it was found. This may help identify the victim.

HEAT INJURY

Aspects

1. Who is the victim?
2. Was the victim alive or dead at the time of the fire?
3. What was the actual cause of the victim's death and was the cause directly related or indirectly related to the fire?
4. Are there any natural diseases or injuries unrelated to the fire which could have caused death or could have been a contributing factor?

5. Was the victim under the influence of drugs or alcohol?
6. What is the manner of death (accident, suicide, homicide)?
7. If the victim was dead at the time of the fire, is there any evidence that the fire may have been a method to destroy or mutilate a homicide victim in order to conceal identity or the true cause and manner of death?
8. Is it possible that the fire was used to destroy or disfigure a dead body in order to perpetrate an insurance fraud?
9. Is there evidence that the decedent was a victim of suicide by other means, having attempted to hide the cause and manner of death by setting fire to the surroundings?
10. Is there evidence of arson with the victim or victims perishing as an unintentional and unforeseen result of a feloniously started blaze?   These questions need to be answered when investigating the aspects of heat injury.

Causes of Injury and Death

1. Flame contact.
2. Severe heating of the body without actual flame contact.
3. Inhalation of carbon monoxide.
4. Inhalation of toxic gases, particularly from burning plastic items.
5. Traumatic injuries due to structural damage of buildings, blast injuries, injuries sustained in escape attempts, injuries due to high pressure hoses, and postmortem injuries due to clearing of the area.

Postmortem Appearance of the Burned Body

1. First, second, and third degree burns with:
   a. Reddened, blistered skin.
   b. Detachment of skin from the hands and feet.
   c. Clothes and firm position against a surface may lessen the heat effects allowing identification of skin color and other skin features.
   d. Gentle rubbing of a burned skin surface may disclose tattooing.
2. Severe burning of body—fourth degree burns.
   a. Usually occurs postmortem.

b. Clothes and hair burning. In an area where oxygen is excluded, shreds of clothing may still be present.

c. Charring of all or part of the body with severe disfigurement, skin splits often with rupture of the stomach wall with protrusion of the intestines, reduced height and weight, burn amputations, contraction of muscles with so-called pugilistic attitude, and usually with well-preserved internal organs.

3. Complete consumption of the body is unusual in most house fires. Chemical fires may cause virtually complete consumption. Small children may be largely consumed.

Chapter 9

DROWNING

DROWNING IS OFTEN CONSIDERED a form of asphyxia. However, actual drowning is very much more involved than lack of air. True asphyxia is said to occur in approximately one in ten drownings. The medical opinions attest that drowning results from closure of the larynx or windpipe. The airway is sealed off and prevents inhalation of water into deeper air passages. Closure of the airway is not detectable at an autopsy due to relaxation of tissues during post-mortem.

Submersion creates a hysteria and the victim struggles to keep their head above the water's surface. The victim attempts to hold their breath until carbon dioxide accumulates in the blood, and reaches a level whereby the victim gasps for breath, inhaling water. Struggling leads to exhaustion. Swallowing water, coughing, vomiting and gradual loss of consciousness proceeds in rapid sequence. The escape of air and the replacement of water continues. Unconsciousness and convulsions associated with gasping precede breathing failure. Irreversible changes in the brain can take place, followed by death in a very short time.

The implication of drowning is usually accidental. Obviously homicide and suicide should always be considered. Duration of submersion is synonymous with establishing the time of death. Many changes in the body depend on the water temperature. Estimation of submersion usually cannot be estimated if duration is greater than one month. The body will sink unless air is trapped in clothing. Due to the weight of the body it will sink quite rapidly. The victim will surface during the decomposition stage. Rigor mortis in drowning has a variable onset due to activity prior to death and water temperature. Livor mortis will be noted in the lower extremities, the face, upper chest, hands, lower arms, feet and calves. The lividity in these areas of the body will be found in an unrestrained body. This will almost always cause the body to float face down, resembling the fetal position. Decomposition also depends on the water temperature and bacteria in the water. Bodies will normally float to the surface in seven to 14 days. Once the body is removed from the water the rate of decomposition is quickened. Remember bodies decompose faster in the air than they do in the water. Adipocere will be more rapid in warmer water.

Some in the medical field believe that a victim can drown in three to five minutes in fresh water, but can take slightly longer in seawater due to salt in the water. Findings are generally similar in both fresh and seawater. However the salt in salt water retards the bacteria and therefore decomposition is slower. Expect to find foam in the nose, or mouth, and water in the lungs and stomach; however, on occasion, none of these items may be found. Findings of foreign material in the mouth, airways, lungs and stomach could be vomit, water plants, or mud. Collapsed lungs filled with water may also be noted.

The circumstances surrounding death is important in establishing the cause of death and for establishing the manner of death. The victim may look the same in a variety of cases no matter how the victim entered the water. The victim could jump, fall, or be pushed and the death investigator will still have the same postmortem findings. Sudden drowning of an accomplished swimmer is not an uncommon event. The swimmer taking deep breaths before a long race can hyperventilate. Once in the water the swimmer can actually pass out or develop unconsciousness and drown. Diving into cold water can also lead to hyperventilation with the same tragic results. Obviously, other deaths can be attributed to diving. Upon entering the pool headfirst the neck or head can be injured, causing a low level of consciousness, allowing inhalation of water.

Other diving-related deaths would be those associated with skin diving or scuba diving. Many of these deaths have contributing factors of equipment failure. Polluted air tanks or lack of air stored in the tanks can be a cause. Inadequate breathing while submerged or air embolism may also be a reason for drowning deaths in the underwater domain. Associated with underwater swimming activities is a health problem termed sudden compression. Sudden compression occurs when underwater divers rise from extended swimming in deep water. Gas bubbles can form in the body from dissolved gases. The formation of gas bubbles can normally be avoided by a slow ascent to the surface of the water. Divers suffering from sudden compression can be successfully treated with expeditious medical treatment. This treatment requires an intake of oxygen and placing the diver into a high pressure chamber.

Most victims that are found in bathtubs either died from a disease, or drowned due to a disease-related unconsciousness. Another incident that the police death investigator needs to investigate is associated with drug overdose. Victims may be found partially or completely submerged in the bathtub after an adverse reaction to a drug overdose. Another instance of drowning, can be associated to cold water drowning. Long duration of immersion in cold water can be extremely fatal, more so than most swimmers understand. The cold water so drastically decreases the metabolic rate that a state of suspended animation develops. The vital functions of the body are slowed and stopped due to the cold water. During this time the body can go longer without oxygen. Frequently, persons are revived after removal from icy waters even though immersion has been longer that the normal three to five minute expectation of drowning taking place. The same length of time under the water, when the water is warmer proves fatal, while cold water drowning does not always result in death. Serious consideration of resuscitation attempts must be made if victims are recovered from cold or icy waters.

HYPOTHERMIA

Exposure of parts of the body such as the nose, ears, fingers and toes may become frozen with the disruption of tissue integrity by ice crystal formation and salt concentration during the freezing process. This can cause extensive circulatory changes and local hypoxia results. Whole body exposure to intense hypothermia may result in fatal circulatory collapse without evidence of freezing any part or, in fact, without the temperatures being below freezing.

It is not uncommon to find children or younger adults who have been found in water or exposed to bitter cold elements that show no vital signs of life. Time of death could be moments to several minutes. Miraculously as it seems, some of these victims have been revived with little or no apparent damage or injury. Other victims have been resuscitated and found to have a small neurological complication. All police and medical responders should understand events related to hypothermia. People's lives can, in some situations, be saved.

The police death investigator must think about postmortem artifacts, injuries that occur after death. Those artifacts are damage done by fish feeding from the body or by propellers of boats. Drowning needs as much investigation as possible. All information developed should be discussed with the pathologist to aid in determining the rightful cause of death.

Case History 1

Two brothers and a friend found an older gentleman while they were out drinking. They thought the old guy had some money. They drove out to the river bridge and there they tied up the old gent with his own shirt that they had cut into strips. The three then robbed the old man of $2.30. The three men pushed the old fellow into the river after tying his hands behind his back. It was in the spring of the year and the river was about 14 feet above flood level. The victim was discovered approximately 40 days later. Homicide by drowning is unusual. Thinking that we may not ever find the victim, one suspect was actually charged before the finding of the body. At the autopsy we discovered $60.00 that the victim had hidden in his sock.

Figure 9.1. Cause of death was due to drowning. Manner of death was due to homicide. The victim's hands had been tied after being robbed. The man was then thrown into the river.

Chapter 10

GUNSHOT WOUNDS

BECAUSE OF THE HIGH NUMBER of deaths, homicides, suicides and accidents associated with gunshot wounds, it is imperative that the police death investigator be well-versed in gunshot wounds. Gunshot wounds occur because of kinetic energy. A projectile needs approximately 200 ft. lb. kinetic energy. This energy is determined by weight and velocity: K.E. = WV2 / 2 g. W is the weight, and V is the velocity, and g represents gravitational acceleration. Velocity is of the greater significance to the formula. K.E. will vary because of type of powder, muzzle fit, barrel length, weight of bullet and caliber.

The bullet, when fired, enters the body causing damage to the outer skin and the tissues it passes through. In smaller caliber weapons the damage is found along the bullet path. In high-powered weapons the damage can be found away from the bullet path. This is due to the body being impacted with this higher velocity. The force of this pressure can produce injuries to organs some distance from the point of entry.

Bullets have a tendency to spiral and tumble producing a larger bullet hole than the size of the bullet. Because of contractions and pulsations this wound will appear to be smaller in seconds after entry. The wound track will still indicate the path that the bullet traveled. It is important to be aware that the bullet does not always travel in a straight line while in the body. A bullet can enter at the top or bottom of the body and actually exit at the opposite end while causing damage throughout the body.

Five Types of Gunshot Wounds

1. Entrance
2. Exit
3. Gutter
4. Re-entry
5. Ricochet

Handgun Ranges

1. Contact
   a. Tight Contact
   b. Loose Contact
2. Close
3. Intermediate
4. Distant

Range Characteristics

CONTACT:	Tight or Loose	Soot in the wound
CLOSE:	12" to 18"	Stippling
INTERMEDIATE:	18" to 36 "	Loose deposit of soot
DISTANT:	36" or more	Lack of soot

Some gunpowders will fly farther and burn faster due to variables such as ball, flake or disc, and the fact that some are cleaner than others. Therefore, range characteristics could be slightly different. Tests with the same weapon and gunpowder should be done whenever possible. Soot or smoke is from gunpowder and can be found, in and around the wound. Tight contact will have soot in the wound. Loose contact will have this soot around the wound. Stippling or tattooing is defined as unburned powder particles. In close range these unburned powder particles can be embedded in the skin around the wound. In distant range lack of soot and stippling should be observed.

Contact wounds are most associated with self-inflicted gunshot wounds, specifically suicide. However, the police death investigator must examine all aspects of the shooting. Gunshot wounds to the head have a blast effect due to gases between the skin and the bone. This causes a stellate or star-shaped wound due to tears in the skin. Soot may not be found on the skin, but will be found in the wound itself. In this type of contact wound, where gases blow the skin outwards from very high velocity, entrance wounds may appear like an exit wound. The exit wound will resemble an entrance wound. This irregular entrance is not the typical damage for an entrance.

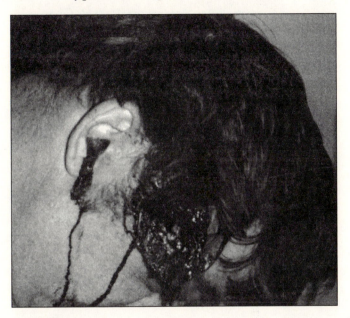

Figure 10.1. (Atypical) Entrance wound associated with contact range. Caused by a build up of gases from a high velocity handgun. Without careful examination this might be considered a typical exit wound.

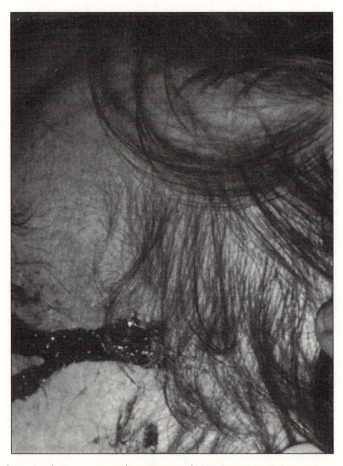

Figure 10.2. (Atypical) Exit wound (see Fig. 10.1). Without careful examination this type of wound could be determined to be a typical entrance wound.

For years we were able to perform a paraffin test on the hands to see if a person fired a gun. Later came the NAA test, Neutron Activation Analysis using 5% nitric acid swabbed on the hands checking for gunpowder residue. These swabs were then analyzed by a flameless atomic absorption spectrophotometry for the presence of lead, barium and antimony from the cartridge primer. Most agencies stopped using these techniques because laboratories were reporting findings on a person's hand of gunpowder from a gun that was shot from across a room. Other tests support that in a room 10 feet by 10 feet it is possible that anyone in the room could conceivably have a positive reaction to having fired a gun.

Shotgun Ranges

1. Cookie cutter	0" to 2'-3'
2. Rat hole	3' to 10'-12'
3. Satellite	12' and beyond

Shotgun barrels have been classified by gauge which is used to describe the caliber of the shotgun. This refers to the choke of the barrel which limits constriction of the bore of the shotgun barrel at the muzzle opening to control shot patterns. Moreover, different chokes produce different shot patterns.

Obviously because of the blast of shot from the shotgun, massive damage from gunshot wounds can be viewed. The pathologist should make every attempt to remove, not only all shot, but also the shot cup and wadding. A unique injury that has been observed from a shotgun wound is the imperfection in the skin that resembles the iron cross. This deformity is seen when the shot cup opens up, striking the body.

A familiar attitude at a death scene is for the emergency personnel to cover the victim with a blanket or sheet. Although a kind gesture, covering a body can be very costly as far as loss of evidence. An excellent example of this loss can be documented in a homicide where the victim was shot once in the eye and then fell to the ground. The victim was then shot in the back four times. The victim was wearing a white overcoat and traces of grease from the bullets could readily be observed. The person responsible for the shooting had kept the bullets in a greasy bag. This bag of greasy bullets was recovered, the weapon was not. By the time the victim was transported to the morgue a blanket had been placed on and taken off the victim numerous times. At the autopsy no grease could be recovered.

Another key element that the death investigator should be aware of is body momentum. Unlike action movies, bodies do not fly across the room when struck by a bullet. The impact of the bullet will not knock you over. The body absorbs the energy of the bullet. The body faces the direction of the momentum.

Classical Gunshot Sites in Suicide

Heart	Temple	Mouth	Forehead

Objectives of the Death Investigator

1. What was the cause of death?
2. How many times was the victim was shot?
3. Determine if wounds are entry or exit.
4. Determination of range of fire.
5. Determination of direction of fire.
6. Evidence recovery.
7. Determination of manner of death, homicide, suicide or accident.

The police death investigator must work very closely with the pathologist at all times.

Unique Findings

Examination of the hands of a shooting victim revealed a strange "L" pattern in soot on the palm of her left hand. The same pattern was found on the back of her right hand. The victim's husband gave a statement that the victim shot herself and the soot on her hands was from having fired the weapon. After careful examination and test firing using graph paper, we were able to reproduce this same "L" pattern. We determined the "L" in soot was created while the victim was attempting to place her hands on the weapon at the time of being shot. The left palm turned in and the right palm turned out had been pressed up against the gun and the cylinder. Like the muzzle flash there was a flash of soot between the cylinder and the barrel of the revolver, creating the "L" shape pattern.

Cylinder Flare

Soot residue that escapes through the gap that exists between the front of the cylinder and the back end of the barrel of revolvers can be seen adjacent to close range and contact entry wounds. The scene investigation, in gunshot cases, should include collection of the weapon, if possible. The weapon, if located, should be made safe using extreme caution not to disturb, contaminate or obliterate any evidence that is present. **Do not allow a loaded or unsafe weapon to be sent to the pathologist or the crime laboratory**. The missiles that exited the body or that were misses should be recovered. Collect all empty spent casings, shot wads or shot cups. Gather any additional

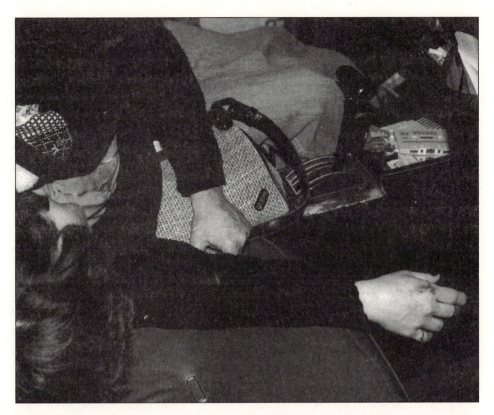

Figure 10.3. Cylinder flare. The victims hands displayed an unusual "L" shaped pattern. This pattern was created by the hands being placed against the cylinder and the barrel of a revolver when fired. This flare originates at that point where the barrel and cylinder meet. (Not the same as muzzle flare.)

live ammo that can be located at the scene. Evidence collection should also include gun-cleaning kits. In all rifle and shotgun cases that might be classified as suicide, be sure to measure the victim's arm and the trigger to muzzle distance.

Chapter 11

CUTTING, STABBING AND BLUNT TRAUMA

CUTTING AND STABBING

THESE TYPES OF WOUNDS are caused by a sharp object that is forced inwards of the body. There are three types of these wounds that the police death investigator should be familiar with. They are incised, stab and chop. The competence to examine and correctly identify the correct type of wound is of great importance in your death investigation. The medical examiner or the pathologist can assist you with these matters of legal importance. Other factors that must be resolved are the number of wounds, the depth of penetration, type of weapon, wound tract and wound angle.

INCISED

Wounds or cuts that are due to contact with a sharp object having been drawn over the skin with enough pressure to produce an injury. These wounds can be various shapes due to the various type of objects used. It is usually difficult to tell much about the instrument that caused the wound. Incised wounds do not penetrate deeply into the body, but merely extend along the skin's surface. Typically self-inflicted injuries are caused by these types of cuts. The term hesitation marks should be considered in all incised wounds; however, this does not exclude homicide. These types of injuries can be caused by cutting or by blunt impact. Blunt force will produce a tear or laceration of the skin. Good scene examination can assist the death investigator in determining the events that occurred.

66

Description

1. Is a cutting wound
2. Usually elongated
3. Usually gaping

PUNCTURE

Wounds that are stab or puncture wounds are due to fairly long and sharp instruments penetrating into the body. It can create danger to the internal organs although the outer skin may not show much of an injury. What appears as a minor wound, to the skin surface, can cause severe internal bleeding and death. Rarely will a stab wound create a bruise. It is more likely that the person holding the knife impacted the body during the stabbing. Stab wounds are more associated with homicide rather than suicide. However, the police death investigator must always consider that deep penetrating wounds can be self-inflicted, unbelievable as it may seem, as some stab wounds are so severe.

Description

1. Is a stab wound
2. Usually penetrating
3. Usually oval

CHOP

Chop wounds are deep and gaping wounds, occasionally involving major structures. These wounds result from heavy and sharp instruments.

Description

1. Caused by a large or heavy object
2. Gaping wound
3. May go as deep as the bone structure

DEFENSE WOUNDS

Occasionally defensive wounds can be observed on a victim. These wounds will be on the hands, arms, feet, legs or perhaps even the shoulders. These wounds are obviously created by the victim attempting to defend himself or herself from the attacker. These defense wounds can be from cutting, stabbing, chopping or from blunt impact. In fights or struggles both the victim and the assailant can have similar wounds. The assailant may attempt to use this in court for his or her defense. Defense wounds are also of value because they indicate that the victim was, at some point, conscious and attempting to resist. Careful examination and study of these types of wounds must be completed along with a comprehensive crime scene investigation.

Case History 1

On the Fourth of July 1976, I became involved in a murder that would take three years to investigate. Fortunately for us we had removed a piece of paneling with a bloody palm print. Three years later the FBI laboratory was able to develop the bloody palm print and make a positive identification to our suspect. The positive print match was of a suspect we had developed in 1976, but could not get enough evidence to file charges. We were aware that he had severely sliced his hand at some time period during the murder. We matched his blood type with blood that we collected at the crime scene. The lab reported the suspect blood type was one in one hundred thousand. However, it was not until we got the print match, that we could make the arrest. To little avail the suspect argued at trial that he was forced to kill the victim because the victim had attacked him with a knife. The scene investigation indicated a fight or struggle, but also showed that a robbery had occurred. The crime scene investigation supported our murder case and not self-defense.

BLUNT TRAUMA

It is sometimes difficult to distinguish between sharp object injury and blunt trauma injury. Both types of injury can produce some similar characteristics. However, a sharp instrument will cut into the tissues. Blunt trauma injury will produce tears or lacerations. There are four categories of injury produced by blunt force; they are bruise or contusions, abrasions, lacerations and bone fractures.

BRUISES/CONTUSIONS

Bruise or contusions are caused by leakage of blood into the skin or tissues or both. Typically the skin is not torn in a bruise or contusion. Bruises can appear quite rapidly and can appear in a pattern. Identification of this pattern will undoubtedly assist the police death investigator in determining the cause or the circumstance of the injury. A fresh bruise will appear reddish or reddish blue in color. The bruise will change in color with age from the reddish color to purple, to green, yellow and into brown. At this point the bruise will start to fade.

Aging of bruises has received mixed comments from the medical community. There are several reasons for the various time schedule of bruising. Infants, elderly or say someone that is diabetic will bruise easier, faster and stay longer than perhaps in a healthy middle-aged man or woman. As with most factors we do have some guidelines that can be followed. The reddish blue color can appear within a few hours of the injury. The purple color can be observed within a week, and the green, yellow and brown color follow very quickly. Total disappearance of the bruise is thought to be within two to four weeks. The bruise examined microscopically will produce a more accurate aging. This can be reported by the pathologist or medical examiner.

Stages

1st Stage	Light Bluish Red	slight swelling noticed in a few hours
2nd Stage	Dark Purple	occurs within a week
3rd Stage	Green	
4th Stage	Yellow	
5th Stage	Brown	lasts about 2-4 weeks

Keep in mind that not all blunt force trauma results in bruising. Bruises may not be observed for several days. Bruising may actually be seen away from the exact point the trauma occurred. Bruising may not be observed in an area where blood has escaped from vessels, such as in lividity. Lastly, remember that the bruise is often larger than the trauma that caused the bruise.

ABRASIONS

Abrasions are due to scraping of the skin and are rarely life-threatening. A pathologist or medical examiner, by incising the abrasion, can determine if the victim was alive when the abrasion was made. This is especially true in cases where the victim might have been restrained or tied up. Hemorrhages that are found in various tissues around the abrasion may be an indication that life was present when the injuries occurred. Unlike bruises that might be found away from the exact point of trauma, abrasions attest to the exact point of blunt force impact.

An abrasion will produce fluid from the tissues or even blood for a day or two. The abrasion will start to heal and become a scab and eventually disappear. There is no absolute rules in aging an abrasion. This healing will be dependent on many variables such as the extent of injury and location. After death the abrasion will dry and could give an appearance of a bruise.

Another unique characteristic of the abrasion is that it can often show the pattern of the object that produced it. Obviously, this pattern can be helpful in determining the attributes of the force that caused the abrasion. This pattern may be located on the skin or even found on the clothing. This pattern may help determine the exact weapon used.

LACERATION

A laceration is tearing from blunt trauma. It should not be interchanged with any other similar injury caused any other way than blunt trauma. Lacerations can have abrasions and bruising surrounding them. The shape of the laceration may indicate the shape of the object that produced the injury.

Lacerations can be caused by being struck and by falling onto a hard surface. The police death investigator must know and understand this. Injuries can be observed that would indicate that the victim was struck, resulting in a laceration. The example that comes to mind, having seen so many instances, is that of an older person who has a heart attack while in the bathroom. The victim falls striking his or her head on the smooth flat surface of the marble top sink.

Occasionally, a laceration can hold additional evidence. Debris or foreign matter from the object that created the injury can reveal how the injury occurred. It is important to note that superficial lacerations may not appear to be significant enough to cause death; however, the victim can be found dead with only this minor injury. External examination may not reveal the severity of the internal damage to the organs, or massive internal bleeding caused by blunt trauma leaving only a small laceration.

BONE FRACTURES

The significance of this information is that sometimes misinterpretations on descriptions of wounds are made in this area. Blunt trauma force can produce an injury of a bone fracture. Different types of injuries will cause different types of fractures. A noted area of interest that relates to injury would be bone fractures that occur from being struck by a vehicle. During investigation questions frequently arise. What type of vehicle was it? How big was the vehicle? Which way was the vehicle traveling? Consideration must also be given to fractures that were produced after death. I have actually witnessed ambulance attendants that caused postmortem fractures when attempting to break rigor mortis to start an IV. They actually fractured a bone in the victim's arm. Rib bones can also be fractured during CPR attempts. As mentioned numerous times before, scene investigation and documentation is crucial. This type of information must be provided by the death investigator to the pathologist or medical examiner. Without this information findings can be inconclusive.

Injuries produced by blunt trauma will be dependent upon how they were caused and what caused it, either by the impact or by the object. There are certain factors that the death investigator must establish. In relationship to the death, when did the injury occur? How the injury occurred, what caused the injury, and what amount of force was needed to produce a particular injury, are all questions that are legally relevant to the investigation.

Remember that an examination of wounds may provide the nature of the instrument, the amount of force used, or the direction of the force. The examination may detect foreign bodies in the wound that are useful in the identification of circumstances.

Chapter 12

ELECTRICAL AND LIGHTNING DEATHS

ELECTRICAL

WHEN AN ELECTRICAL CURRENT passes through a human body, a wide variety of effects can be produced and observed. Injury from electrocution can be as insignificant as a muscle spasm up to and including death. Strangely, death can result from electricity passing through the body without showing any signs of burns. Yet, just the opposite can also be observed. An individual may be severely burned from having come in contact with electricity and death may not result.

Death is caused by a high voltage of electricity passing throughout the body and affecting the heart or brain. Additionally, large amounts of heat that is produced by the body may also be a contributing factor to the onset of death. Of great significance is that portion of the body that the current passes through. For example, should the current pass through the heart, the failure of the heart results in death. Should the current pass through a limb like the leg, then only the leg will be severely damaged. As mentioned, the body may produce large amounts of heat. This build-up of heat can be a cause of death or produce other injuries. That portion of the body that comes into direct contact with the electrical current may have burns where the current actually entered the body. Additionally, the body can be burned where the current exits the body.

In lower voltage electrocutions death may not occur instantaneously. Normally in this type of electrocution the heart beat is affected by a change in rhythm caused by the electrical current. Called auricular fibrillation, low voltage electrocution causes the heart to fail, shutting down the supply of blood to the brain, resulting in unconsciousness. Life in this circumstance can be saved if recognized quickly enough, and by administering artificial respiration. During cardiac defibrillation, an electrical current flow used to put the heart in rhythm is enormous; however, it is only operated for a short duration.

The death investigator must also keep in mind that a victim does not necessarily need to come into direct contact with an electrical current to be electrocuted. Many objects that we touch every day can become conductors of electricity. One example of a conductor that we encounter is water. In severe storms where wind and rain are produced, electrical power lines can be knocked down, perhaps even fall in a small puddle of water. Coming in contact with the water can produce electrocution although the victim never touched the power line. How about the faulty light in the swimming pool? A swimmer can be electrocuted by placing a foot in the pool to test the temperature of the water yet never coming into direct contact with the electricity.

Likewise, machinery and construction equipment can become conductors of electricity when a part of the machinery comes in contact with a power line or other source of electricity. Thus, the operator and any one else touching the machinery may be electrocuted.

Electrocution Key Points

1. Causes interruption of the heart or brain.
2. Good opportunity for resuscitation.
3. Body must be part of circuit between power and ground.
4. Body is a conductor of electricity.
5. Occasionally, the better the contact, the lower the burn.
6. Longer contact can produce more damage.
7. Higher voltage is more dangerous.
8. May initially survive and death occur later.
9. May not be able to see any marks of electrocution.

LIGHTNING

Lightning strikes the ground more than eight million times a day. Worldwide, more than one thousand people are killed each year from lightning. Some 300 to 400 people, in the United States are struck by lightning every year. Amazingly most people struck by lightning will survive.

There is no absolute method to avoid being struck by lightning; however, there are some things that a person can do that might help. Stay clear of trees, get away from water, and avoid metal objects like golf clubs. Other items that should be avoided, during an electrical storm are electrical appliances, water lines and other plumbing, and telephone lines. Automobiles may help to avoid lightning strikes to some degree, but this is not a totally effective method. Lightning can and has struck and killed occupants of vehicles.

Unlike electrical deaths, victims of lightning are struck by a current up to twenty million volts for only a brief moment. A lightning strike resembles effects from a high voltage electrocution. Electrical current from lightning passes through the body's internal electrical circuits involving the heart and the brain. This can occur without evidence of injury to the surface of the body, or with only very minor injuries. It is rare to observe severe burning from a lightning strike. A tremendous amount of heat, fifty thousand degrees, can be produced from a body in a lightning strike. Metal objects on victims have actually melted, yet the body showed little or no evidence of any burning. The skin of lightning strike victims may appear blue. Large amounts of blood may be found internally due to hemorrhaging.

One noticeable effect of lightning strike is a fern-like pattern, referred to as LICHTENBERG'S FLOWERS, that can be observed in the upper portions of the body. This can be seen across the upper back and shoulders and in the upper trunk area of the front of the body. Formerly, these plant-like designs seen on the body were thought to be patterns of the nearby plants and trees. Still an unresolved question pertaining to the fern-like patterns is whether this pattern develops at the instant of the strike, or is something that develops postmortem. Generally accepted is the thought that this pattern is caused by the breakdown of red cells within the skin and blood entering the tissues. This fern pattern may be the only indication that a victim was struck by lightning, and therefore, the body must be carefully examined whenever lightning is suspected as the cause of death.

Another important fact for the police death investigator to be aware of is that a person may die from what is thought to be a lightning strike; however, the person was not actually struck by lightning. When lightning strikes the ground, expanded or expelled air can toss the victim for some distance producing injuries sufficient to cause death. Expect to find evidence of the victim's clothing having been torn, shoes that appear to have been removed. Whether it be from electrocution or lightning strike, it is crucial to check all of the victim's clothing. Electricity upon leaving the body can blow out parts of the body and clothing as well. In some instances, victims of lightning strikes may appear like victims of vehicle pedestrian crashes.

Lightning Key Points

1. Unpredictable
2. Extremely high voltage
3. May hit other objects first, then strike body
4. May disrupt clothing
5. Fern-like patterns
6. Shoulders and feet are where electrical path normally travels

Chapter 13

TRAFFIC CRASHES

TRAFFIC CRASHES ARE THE LEADING cause of all accidental deaths and all deaths of persons under 25 years of age. Due to this high number of traffic crash deaths, the increase in caseload can present additional problems for many police agencies. One reason that problems occur in death cases related to traffic crashes is because they may be under litigation for many years before a final disposition is obtained. Additionally, most traffic crashes are left to the uniform, or patrol division to investigate. A police officer on the beat, may do an excellent job investigating vehicle accidents, however, serious problems can arise in those accidents where the crash becomes fatal.

It is of significant value to law enforcement and the community to insure that the traffic crash is properly and completely investigated. The police have a responsibility to the innocent. It has often been said that police officers are gatherers of the facts. In some instances this concept is enough; however, in death cases an investigator with a background in death investigation should be involved in the investigation and reconstruction process of fatality accidents. It is crucial that accidents that result in death are carefully investigated to insure that criminal and civil justice is fulfilled.

On a positive viewpoint, the auto construction industry, for the most part are currently meeting or exceeding vehicle safety standards set by the government. Also, the National Highway Traffic Safety Administration (NHTSA) has set out guidelines for traffic safety. These guidelines include safety standards that relate to doors, doorlocks, energy absorbent steering wheels, dashboards, front and rear bumpers, front seat airbags, side door airbags, and the use of seat belts have all helped to reduce the number of deaths.

Figure 13.1. Traffic crash involving a large tractor trailer. The one-vehicle accident that resulted in the death of the driver of the truck had to be reconstructed to determine exactly what had happened to cause the crash. Note the skid marks on the roadway.

However, even with all of these safety features, traffic crash deaths continue to occur. Some of the safety features can be a contributing factor to injury or death. Seat belts have been a source of injury in instances where the impact force is extremely high; however, being thrown from a vehicle, increases the occupants potential for fatal injury by more than five times. Airbags have also produced severe and fatal injury upon inflation. Deaths of infants placed in a car seat in the front seat have been attributed to the inflation of the front seat airbag.

Traffic crash death investigation is at the top of the types of cases that require, no command teamwork. Only by a concentrated team effort of the accident investigator, accident reconstruction officer, death investigator, emergency medical personnel, pathologist and coroner, is it possible to establish pertinent and relevant facts of the crash. It is only by the combined efforts of these professionals that a competent investigation can be completed.

Only within the past few years has the accident reconstruction officer (ARO) surfaced as one of the most substantial elements in the investigation of traffic crashes. It is unfortunate that all law enforcement agencies in the country cannot have their own accident reconstruction officer. Realizing this is not possible, it is important to note most larger cities, counties, and state police agencies have a qualified ARO that, upon a request can assist you with your accident investigation. Understanding the contributions that the ARO can add to an investigation, I began including a block of instruction in my death investigation classes about accident reconstruction. I was fortunate to enlist the expertise of Illinois State Trooper Daniel Derenzy to instruct on the subject. Trooper Derenzy, a certified accident reconstruction officer, holds a Bachelor of Science Degree in Nursing and is a member of the Illinois Association of Technical Accident Investigators (IATAI). IATAI certifies sworn law enforcement personnel nationwide as accident reconstruction officers. Their web site can be located at www.iatai.org.

There has been such an interest in this type of instruction, that Trooper Derenzy now teaches an eight-hour block of instruction on accident reconstruction. An ARO can add a new dimension and wealth of information to a traffic crash investigation. It is imperative to prove what happened, not just report what you think happened. It is of vast importance that the police death investigator seek out those in other areas of law enforcement and the community that have an expertise that can assist you.

ASSIGNMENT

An initial step in the traffic crash death investigation is to establish what category of assignment each victim falls into. There are four of these assignments: (1) driver, (2) passenger, (3) pedestrian, and (4) unknown. All of these assignments can be extremely difficult to determine. Even at those times when you have survivors, the question of truth will always arise. As difficult as it may be, it is imperative to establish an assignment for each person. There are things that you can do to help establish a victim's location during the traffic crash. Check the positions of the victims in the vehicle (unless the vehicle rolled over). Check the soles of their shoes for brake pedal impressions, clothing, fibers, blood, hair, and fingerprints that might be matched with specific areas of the vehicle. The pattern of injury or trauma may also provide an assignment or location.

WITNESSES

Witnesses can be helpful, however, they can also create big problems. You must always be aware of the single survivor who implicates someone else as the driver. Also of concern is the sober driver who may change positions with an intoxicated driver, especially in vehicle pedestrian accidents. It is not unusual for a witness involved in the traffic crash, to have posttraumatic loss of memory. The ideal witness is the person outside the vehicle who is unrelated to anyone involved in the traffic crash, and who has no interest in the outcome of the accident investigation.

SCENE INVESTIGATION

When considering the use of a certified accident reconstruction officer, nothing that relates to the scene should be moved or removed unless absolutely necessary. The distance that a car battery flew may not seem important to the death investigator, however it can be extremely crucial to the accident reconstruction officer to prove exactly when the chain of events occurred.

If an ARO is not going to be utilized, or cannot get to a scene until a later time, you must preserve, note and collect vital evidence. Scene measurements should be taken. Measure everything that can be measured. The distance of the tire marks, the distance of items or person thrown or ejected from the vehicle, glass fragments, and anything else that can be observed that relates to the accident. Carefully and accurately record these items and measurements. Take photographs of all pertinent items, objects, victims, vehicles, and the overall accident scene. If the traffic crash occurs at night, take pictures at that time and then go back during daylight hours and take additional photographs.

The collection of physical evidence should include glass or glass fragments, bloodstains, personal effects, shoes, clothing fragments, detached vehicle parts and headlamp and taillight bulbs. As in many collection of evidence situations, it is better to collect it now and not need it, than to not collect it and need it later.

In handling the body at the scene it has been stated throughout this handbook to place a white sheet under the victim and place the sheet and the body in a body bag for transportation to the morgue. Any clothes on the body need to be left on the body. Additionally, items of clothing found at the scene should be packaged separately. These items should be taken to the autopsy to match items to a particular victim or other items of clothing. Once your evidence has been collected from the vehicle(s) and from the scene of the traffic crash, you may want to have a vehicle inspected by a competent auto mechanic for mechanical problems that might be a contributing factor to the accident. The mechanic may be able to provide specific information that might relate to the steering or the brakes of a vehicle, or something that may be of significance about the tires.

CAUSES AND FACTORS

There may be one cause of a traffic crash, yet that one cause may have several contributing factors. High speed, reckless driving, or just plain inexperience are other causes that should be considered, along with equipment failure such as brakes, steering, or loss of power. Other factors may be such things as: alcohol, drug intoxication, or heart attack. Environmental conditions such as rain, snow, ice and in some instances carbon monoxide poisoning, could also be a cause of an accident.

It is not uncommon for victims of natural death to actually have a collision with another vehicle or object. Frequently, the victim can pull to the side of the road before an accident occurs. However, if death does occur, little or no damage is done to the car, and the victim does not show significant signs of severe trauma. The same findings may be indicated in deaths brought on by carbon monoxide poisoning from a faulty exhaust system; little or no damage to the victim or the vehicle is observed. The competent auto mechanic can provide important information about this particular defect.

PEDESTRIANS

All too often the traffic crash investigations involve a pedestrian where the driver of the vehicle drives away. Persons struck by moving vehicles with any force have a low rate of surviving. The old and the very young are obviously more susceptible to severe injury from being struck. In any instance, the mere force of the impact can throw the victim. Lower extremity injuries and head trauma is common. The force of being struck can also result in extreme internal trauma.

Known as the hit-and-run accident, this type of case is quite often difficult to investigate and prove. It is crucial to carefully examine the scene and the victim for any evidence that might be left by the suspect vehicle. Evidence that may have been left could be minute or non-existent. When a suspect vehicle is located, this same careful examination of the vehicle must be performed. Additionally, careful measurements of the vehicle must be taken, including the height from the ground to the bumper of the vehicle. The bumper is commonly where the impact with the pedestrian occurs. It is dependent on the speed and the relationship of the positioning of the pedestrian and the vehicle as to whether the victim is pushed away from the vehicle, thrown up in the air or thrown over the vehicle.

Obviously, if the victim is pushed away from the impact there is only the initial point of contact that may provide evidence on the victim or on the vehicle. If the pedestrian is lifted or thrown upwards at impact, there may be additional damage to the upper surface of the suspect vehicle. Lastly, the vehicle may simply run over the pedestrian, doing only minimal damage to the undercarriage of the vehicle. If a hit-and-run suspect vehicle is to be examined, a complete examination of the vehicle from front to back and top to bottom must be performed.

A question that often arises in traffic crash-related deaths, is whether or not an autopsy should be performed on the victims, and if so, which victim. It is not always necessary to perform an autopsy on each victim from the traffic crash. The initial findings from the accident investigation can help determine who should or who should not have an autopsy. For an example, a small child placed in a car seat in the rear of the vehicle should not needlessly undergo an autopsy, but certainly the driver of the vehicle or the pedestrian should be considered. The resolution concerning a postmortem examination should be based upon an evaluation of importance by the investigative team. If a decision is made not to have an autopsy on a particular fatality the victim should at least have a comprehensive external examination that includes complete photographs, x-rays and toxicology.

The results of a traffic crash investigation goes far beyond a conclusion of what happened, which in itself can often be quite difficult. Actually, the results of your investigation will be of great interest to a great many people and groups. The findings will hold personal, civil and criminal attention. The family will certainly have a personal interest in your findings. Others that may be impacted by your conclusion could be the owners of the vehicle, employers of drivers, auto manufacturers, insurance companies, the medical profession and our court systems. Moreover, the future safety of anyone that gets into an automobile and ventures out on our streets and highways will be impacted from the investigative outcome of each traffic crash. Your investigative efforts are very important and must not be taken lightly. The role of the police death investigator is very important and should not be underestimated.

You must also consider not all traffic crashes that result in death should be considered as vehicular accidents. The police death investigator should be cognizant that a motor vehicle can be used to help facilitate a suicide or a homicide. During the course of your investigation, you must be looking for any observation that does not appear to be right or that creates a suspicion. Those observations may include no brake or skid marks, eyewitnesses who say the vehicle accelerated before the crash, a vehicle that strikes another object "head-on" or "dead center," or the findings of an accelerator pedal imprint on the sole of a shoe.

One-car accidents where there is no apparent cause should be thought of as suspicious. The lack of mechanical problems or when the environmental conditions are not a factor should also be considered questionable. Vehicles that are pulled onto railroad tracks in front of trains and stopped should be considered questionable. The concern of suicide with the use of an automobile must not be limited to just the occupant of the vehicle. Consider the pedestrian that intentionally jumps into the path of an oncoming automobile or train. This form of suicide can obviously be very successful.

Homicide by vehicle although uncommon, must be contemplated. Remember that the same rules apply in a traffic crash death investigation as in any other death investigation. It is better to work the case down from homicide to suicide, to accident, and then to natural. What initially comes to mind are those situations where the pedestrian is deliberately struck, causing death. Other situations in which the automobile can serve in homicide is the vehicle that runs another person off the road, off a cliff, or into the water. This scenario can be further complicated when the victim in the vehicle may have been unconscious or already dead before leaving the road. The police death investigator must never take anything for granted. It is not what you think, it is what you can prove that matters.

Another use of the vehicle as a mechanism for murder is accomplished when an exploding device is attached to the vehicle. These devices are connected to the ignition to explode when the vehicle is started or wired, or to the brake lights to activate when the victim pushes the brake pedal. These types of explosions can be achieved by many other means. Any explosive device can create and produce these types of fatal results.

Chapter 14

DEATHS DUE TO COCAINE

ONE HAS TO WONDER how many cocaine-related deaths were mis-interpreted as far back as the 1970s when my career first began. That time when cocaine was the recreational drug of choice. Police death investigators and pathologists alike were unaware that some deaths were related to cocaine. Today we are more familiar with the term cocaine excited delirium or fatal respiratory collapse. Because of low levels of cocaine the drug was not suspected as lethal cocaine intoxication.

It was not until the early 1980s that I first became interested in cocaine-related deaths. By that time many studies were being conducted across the country. Some statistics were showing an increase in these cocaine-related deaths rate, as much as five times higher from 1980 until 1990. Such a drastic increase can be attributed to availability, increase of purity, and an increase of users of the drug. During the past decade the death investigators and the medical profession have seen a drastic increase in deaths that can be attributed to cocaine. Some pathologists feel that the death rate related to cocaine may be higher than reported, simply because not enough information has been learned.

Cocaine was first introduced into the United States as an anesthetic in the 1850s. It causes vasoconstriction, narrows the blood vessels and stimulates both the central nervous system and the cardial vascular system. Additionally, cocaine manipulates the brain and raises blood pressure and heart rate. There is an increasing awareness that cocaine can cause psychosis, hyperthermia, convulsions and sudden death. The government passed the Harrison Act between 1913 and 1914 outlawing cocaine and stated in 1927 that cocaine was gone from the country. However, in the 1960s and 1970s cocaine was back and being used recreationally.

Due to a sharper awareness of cocaine-related deaths, numerous similarities in these types of death are being documented. Information shows that victims exhibit signs of disturbance, became quite physical, developed paranoia and had unexplained strength. Furthermore, the victims experienced hyperthermia and disrobed. Additional information indicated that the victims had an affinity for breaking glass. The obvious reaction to this type of behavior is, of course, intervention by the police. It is without question that the police will have to become physical to restrain the individual. To say the least, it will take numerous police personnel to subdue the person making use of all available restraints.

Cocaine excited delirium deaths have created a magnitude of problems for police departments across the country. Sudden and unexpected deaths due to cocaine poisoning are becoming a serious problem for police officers throughout the country. If the correct cause and manner of death is not determined in these types of deaths, police agencies may even become legally liable for the death. Police and medical emergency personnel need to be aware of the possibility for sudden and expected death due to excited delirium. With this situation in mind, there must not be any delay in transporting the subject to the hospital. It is imperative that the cardiovascular system is constantly monitored and reported to hospital staff while enroute. All hospital physicians and medical staff should be made fully aware that a cocaine excited delirium case is being brought in. They should be prepared to handle the adverse reaction and cardiac symptoms that can be expected. Only in those situations that prompt diagnosis and treatment are given can any expectation of survival be expected.

As seen in cocaine excited delirium, the victim will, at some point after struggling with the police, have sudden tranquillity indicating the problem is over. Unfortunately, this is just where the problems really begin. When sudden tranquillity comes, death may follow. Documentation of this type of death indicated that after the victim becomes tranquil, respiratory arrest developed within a few minutes to an hour or more.

Because of this increasing problem in society, it obviously equates to a serious problem for all law enforcement and medical personnel. It is with the utmost importance, that the men and women in these professions be able to recognize cocaine excited delirium and be prepared to deal with it at the onset. Preplanning is paramount to handle these types of situations before there is a death. Not only should police and medical personnel be aware of this problem, but the community should also be educated to the potential problems of cocaine use. Most drug prevention programs educate on the use of drugs and its effect generally; however, some law enforcement agencies still do not understand the full impact of deaths due to cocaine.

The first responder must recognize what they see and understand what they are dealing with. The victim of cocaine excited delirium can show any or all of the following signs: agitation, paranoia, confusion, aggressiveness, violence, dilated pupils, increased body temperature, unexpected strength, hyperthermia, the urge to remove clothing and possibly break glass. The victim can be very combative, may have convulsions or go into a seizure. The first responder, once this is recognized, must ask and receive as much assistance that is available. The use of mace or stun guns has been shown to be ineffective. The use of nets with quick connection straps is strongly suggested as a means of securing the individual as quickly as possible.

First responders should also be watching for the subject to become tranquil, once this occurs the victim can die within a very short time. Cocaine poisoning or overdose can be quite sudden, frequently followed by seizure and respiratory collapse. Some instances of death have come as quickly as 45 minutes after police were called. Should cocaine be considered as the cause of excited delirium, medical personnel must be given that information immediately. This will enable them to provide prompt diagnosis and appropriate medical attention to assist in preventing sudden respiratory collapse and death.

Cocaine can be snorted, injected or smoked. It is necessary to gather any evidence of drug usage. Check the nose for evidence of snorting and check the body for needle marks. A cocaine injection mark will appear greatly different in comparison to a heroin injection. A heroin user will have the familiar "tracks" along and away from the vein. The cocaine injection mark will appear as a needle mark, followed by a circular pattern of clear skin, followed by a circular pattern of blood or bruising under the skin. Once the cocaine enters the body it will break down. It is often difficult to tell just how the cocaine might have been ingested. It must also be understood that cocaine in the victim can deteriorate and low levels or no levels may be found.

Once death has occurred in a person believed to be the victim of a cocaine overdose, several important items must be considered. It has been suggested by the medical community that cocaine by deterioration can disappear in as little as four hours. Obviously, it would be very difficult to argue cocaine overdose when there is no evidence of cocaine in the body. Additional information indicated that the brain seems to provide excellent tissue for determination of presence of cocaine. However, cocaine will also disappear from these tissues unless frozen. A minus 80 degrees will stop the deterioration. Another important factor that needs to be accomplished is to see that blood samples are taken in a gray top tube. This should be preserved in sodium fluoride and refrigerated to minimize the deterioration. Although not readily available the use of liquid nitrogen will snap freeze any tissue samples and preserve them.

When evidence of cocaine can be found in the body, the levels of the drug may be quite low. There is no determinant lethal level of cocaine. It can be difficult to understand, especially by family and friends of the victim, why death occurred. It may be argued that the victim never used cocaine, or ingested no more than the usual amount, or had done this many times before and never had a problem. These are all classic examples of when this excited delirium will occur. Death can be brought about for the first-time user, as well as someone having used the drug in the past for many years. Unfortunately, family members do not understand this situation. They only realize that the police fought with their loved one and the cause of death must have been from fighting since a large number of police officers were needed to subdue the person.

Case History 1

In the summer of 1989, a 33-year-old male entered a neighborhood bar, one he had been to many times in the past. He began pounding on the bar demanding a drink. He was shouting that he wanted some liquor and was not being served. It was obvious that the subject was now quite agitated and began breaking the bar glasses. Four other patrons along with the bar owner attempted to restrain and remove the now fully enraged man. A call was placed to the local police explaining that the subject was now out of control and continuing to destroy the bar. Several police units were dispatched with the first units arriving in minutes after the call. The subject, when confronted by the police, displayed an unusual amount of unexpected strength. The subject fought with six uniformed police officers for several minutes before eventually being taken down to the floor. The victim was struck several times with night sticks across his body while fighting with the police officers. Once on the floor the victim was handcuffed. The victim was transported to the hospital. Like the police, the victim had suffered numerous cuts from the broken bar glasses. Upon arrival at the hospital the victim was pronounced dead. The victim's family, certain that their loved one had died from being struck by the police officers, filed a wrongful death suit. The county and the city each paid an undisclosed amount to settle the suit.

Case History 2

In 1993, an identical situation occurred. Just as the first man had done, the second person became violent and fought with the police. Upon arrival at the hospital he also died. Because of the cuts and bruises his family was sure that his death was due to being hit by the police. An autopsy was performed. While speaking with the pathologist about the death, it was learned that he had never heard of cocaine excited delirium. In August of 1993, the pathologist released his findings as to cause of death. Immediate cause of death was cardiopulmonary arrest due to or as a consequence of excited delirium due to or as a consequence of cocaine overdose. There were no settlements and the wrongful death suit was dismissed in this case.

Deaths related to cocaine are not always cases where the victim was attempting to use the drug. There are cases where victims of cocaine overdose had swallowed condoms filled with cocaine. The condoms can rupture causing acute fatal cocaine poisoning. Evidence that the police death investigator will likely find will be similar to a case involving ingested cocaine. Wet towels indicative of hyperthermia are often found. Hyperthermia is directly related to cocaine poisoning. Hyperthermia, induced by cocaine, may elevate the body temperature to 108 degrees or higher. The body will be unusually warm and may bring about postmortem rigidity soon after death because of the high temperatures associated with hyperthermia. Enema paraphernalia and laxatives may also be observed, as the victim would be attempting to pass the cocaine-filled condoms.

In all cases expect the victim to exhibit bizarre and aggressive behavior, paranoia, panic, violence, shouting and fear. The suspect will show signs of unexpected strength. The suspect will also become suddenly quiet and give an indication of respiratory arrest. The failure will come on quite quickly and normally before arrival at the hospital.

An immediate indication that should alert the law enforcement community to the potential cocaine-induced excited delirium is the observance of paranoia, violence, and bizarre behavior. High body temperature and seizures will accompany this behavior. The continuation of violence or thrashing after having been restrained will undoubtedly lead to sudden tranquillity. Heart failure will certainly follow.

Cocaine Reaction

1. Euphoria
2. Exaggerated alertness
3. Perspiration
4. Tension
5. Anxiety
6. Lack of sleep
7. Agitation
8. Paranoia
9. Unexpected strength
10. Increased body temperature

Chapter 15

INFANT DEATH

THE INVESTIGATION OF INFANT DEATH will fall into one of three categories, natural, accidental, or homicide. Obviously, suicide is not considered a factor until older childhood has developed. The death investigation of an infant can be more different than that of an adult. The investigator will have to deal with very strong emotions. These strong emotions are not only manifested by the parents, but can also be apparent in the death investigator. This type of death can be very difficult to investigate due to the high level of emotions that can overwhelm the police death investigator. All too often the investigator can demonstrate an inconsistent course of action. Some police death investigators may not feel that the death of a child is as significant or as important as the death of an adult. This type of attitude can be as injurious to the investigation as being too emotionally involved. In any instance, the investigator must be careful not to project any indication of guilt or from wrongful accusations.

The police death investigator must conduct this type of investigation with professional demeanor. This professional conduct must be displayed throughout the length of the investigation, which includes interaction with the family and dealing with the media. Media interest in this type of investigation can fuel a public outcry for immediate investigative results, attempting to force the police to make a quick arrest in murder cases of little children. Interest by the media may also pressure the police to provide or release pertinent case information. Law enforcement's logic of thinking is that if something is given to the media they will back off. This is not ever the case in these matters.

During the death investigation of an infant, suspicion of foul play should always be considered. As with all cases, work the death as a murder. Then work the case as accidental. When both of the these two

90

possibilities have been ruled out, then natural death can be considered.

However suspicious, the communication between the investigator and the family can be extremely critical. False accusations made to the family can produce severe psychological damage. The last thing that parents who just lost their baby need is to be wrongfully accused of the death of their baby. Additionally, parents should not be made to feel guilty that they did something wrong to bring about the death of the infant when the cause of death is natural. Moreover, the investigation only gets compounded if the family decides to no longer cooperate or elects to get an attorney.

The death of an infant requires special investigative skills and expertise. Recognizing and understanding evidence developed at the scene is very important. These discoveries may be the only indication as to how the infant died. Just as important, the police death investigator must work closely with the medical examiner or pathologist.

In infants from birth to one year, natural disease is the most common cause of death. This natural disease also includes SIDS, or Sudden Infant Death Syndrome. Most diseases can be determined by examination, while others strike too quickly. Infants older than one year are more susceptible to accidental death. These types of accidents may include suffocation, poisoning, falls, or traffic crashes. In these types of deaths, as much physical evidence as possible must be collected. This evidence would include cribs, blanket and pillows, stuffed animals and other toys, household liquids and compounds, and car seats.

Infants at any age can be a victim of homicide. Homicide of an infant or small child is not uncommon. The death of a child is usually caused by a parent or some other person in charge of caring for the infant. The death of the infant may be the first time for any type of abuse; however, the death investigator should always check for any past history of abuse or neglect. The medical examiner or pathologist may also be able to provide additional evidence of prior mistreatment.

SUDDEN INFANT DEATH SYNDROME

Since SIDS is a disease that accounts for most deaths in infants between birth and one year of age, the police death investigator needs to have some knowledge in this area. SIDS is unpredictable and perhaps more importantly, unpreventable. In SIDS cases, the infant is placed in its bed for an afternoon nap or for a night of sleep. Later, a parent finds the dead child. The child may still be in a normal sleeping position or perhaps turned over.

Recently, information made available regarding SIDS indicates that victims are found dead with their noses and mouths turned into the bedding on which they sleep. Accordingly, these bedding items are softer and limit carbon dioxide dispersal, causing more rebreathing of exhaled gases. Rebreathing of exhaled gases may explain some deaths associated with SIDS. Other considerations must also be given as to whether some bedding might retain carbon dioxide.

As a police death investigator charged with investigating this mechanism of death, he or she must not only conduct an investigation, but should also make every effort to help the emotional security of the family. Often the family will blame themselves, believing that the death was a result of something they did or did not do. Police officers are not social workers; however, they must show a great deal of human compassion when working this type of case.

CHILD ABUSE OR NEGLECT

The appearance of the abused or neglected infant will obviously be different than a child who dies of a normal disease. The observable indications would be things such as: signs of injury, broken bones, bruises, burns, cuts, scars, or other wounds or trauma. The neglected child may also show signs of malnutrition. It is important to check other infants in the family for any of the aforementioned indicators.

One or both parents can be responsible for the abuse. Keep in mind that it is possible for one parent to be the abuser and the other parent be totally unaware of the mistreatment to the infant. This situation may also occur when the infant is left with a childcare provider. The parents may be totally unaware of the abuse or neglect. The death investigator may find that the parents or childcare provider cannot provide a plausible story as to how injuries occurred.

It is the responsibility of the death investigator to determine the manner of death when homicide is suspected. Infants may be victims of homicide that would not occur in older children or adults. An example would be the shaking of a baby. This shaking can causes serious brain damage or even death. The investigator must determine if the death of the infant was brought about by an intentional or an unintentional act. Always gather as much information and evidence as possible. Comparison and evaluation of this information is significant. Additionally, provide the medical examiner or pathologist with all investigative findings. Again, infant death can be natural, accidental, or a homicide.

Extreme care must be exercised when investigating the circumstances of a possible child abuse or neglect-related death. No other cause of death is so important for the police death investigator to conduct a complete and comprehensive investigation. Children can be killed in such discriminating methods that only by thorough investigation can an appropriate determination as to the cause and manner of death be made. You must go to the scene of an infant death as soon as possible, even if the infant's body is no longer present. If the child is present, note the position the body is in, if the body was found in this position or if it has been moved. Determine how the child was found and how the child was dressed or covered with any item or object. Make a written description of any presence of rigor mortis, livor mortis, vomit or blood. Note the environmental temperature and conditions. Note any obvious attempts to change the scene. Take photographs as soon as possible of the infant and the environment. As most infant deaths occur in the home, it is important to check the entire home and not just the immediate area where the baby was found. Check the overall condition and appearance of the house. Check for the presence of other siblings in the home and note their appearance.

Obviously the difference in size of an infant and an adult is indisputable. It should be just as evident that the adult does not need any type of weapon to injure a child. Most injuries to the infant are blunt trauma, contusions or bruises, abrasions, or lacerations. As mentioned earlier, due to the size relationship of the infant and the adult there are various types of violence that can produce death in a child that would have no or very little effect if done to an older person. Shaking, squeezing, or even a smack can produce injuries that can result in death.

The most common cause of infant death in child abuse victims is head trauma. There may or may not be external injury about the head.

The second most common cause of infant death from abuse is due to injury to the chest or stomach area that causes severe injury to the internal organs. As you can imagine, a knee to the chest of a small infant can easily cause fatal injuries. The face, teeth, cheeks, lips and frenulum are all areas where child abuse can be observed. Burns on the infant may be accidental, but in the abused child they are an intentional cruelty. Burns are not only produced by an open flame; burns can also be found from placing the infant in water that is too hot. Check the water temperature in the home. Placing a child in scalding water can only be interpreted as intentional. Other abuse or neglect may be the result of denying nutritional or medical requirements. Infants and smaller children have needs that only an adult can provide. The failure to properly care for an infant may produce death that can be considered as homicide.

Child abuse, also known as Battered Child Syndrome, refers to the direct and repeated physical or mental abuse or the neglect of a small child. Today the medical profession and social service organizations are more aware of this type of abuse and can react more quickly than in earlier days. The abuser can be a parent, a baby-sitter, a boyfriend, or even a sibling, with the abuse generally directed towards the youngest child.

ABORTION

It must be stated that the information and material contained in this section of the chapter is neither in support or in opposition of legalized abortion. It has been prepared for the knowledge, education, and understanding by the police death investigator. The police death investigator must not let his or her own opinions influence their investigation. There are many forms of child abuse or neglect imposed on children. Those types include child abandonment, child endangerment, drug abuse and drug addiction of the newborn. Again, for the purpose of this material abortion is listed as another form of abuse or neglect.

Elective Abortion: (Know your state laws)

In cases where the fetus is alive and then dies or the mother dies, the death should be investigated by the police.

Spontaneous Abortion: (Miscarriage)

Abortion occurs naturally, it is not due to interference or external agents or drugs. If death occurs outside the hospital, it should be investigated.

Therapeutic Abortion: (Doctor/Patient decision)

Hospital-induced abortion to save the life or health of the pregnant mother. Referred to as justifiable abortion, it may be performed after sexual assaults.

Accidental Abortion: (Police must investigate)

An abortion is brought on by an accident or other external trauma. It is necessary to establish two standards to prove that death was related to the trauma. Both standards must be proven.

Two Rules of Accidental Abortion

1. Proof must be established that the pregnancy was normal without any complications prior to the trauma. This can be accomplished by past medical history that reflects the health of the mother and the growth of the fetus. An autopsy will indicate if the fetus was normally developed by growth of the fetus and organs. The autopsy would also show that the fetus had no congenital defects, infections or disease prior to the trauma.

2. Within minutes or hours of the trauma the abortion or events leading up to an abortion would have to take place. It may take hours or days before the fetus is actually aborted. However, any indication of the forthcoming abortion such as bleeding, or other birthing complications must take place within minutes to hours after the determined time of the trauma. Prime examples of the traumatic abortion

are vehicle crashes or an instance where the mother is attacked or beaten. This same type of abortion can occur simply by the mother falling. Again, traumatic abortion cases must be investigated completely.

Examples of Differences Between SIDS and Child Abuse

SIDS	*ABUSE/NEGLECT*
No sign of injury	Visible signs of injury
Natural looking	Broken bones
Lividity appropriate	Bruises
Quick rigor (2-3 Hrs)	Burns or cuts
Well-developed baby	Head trauma
Other siblings appear healthy	Scars, welts or other wounds
Parents story: Baby was fine when put down for a nap.	* Parents story just does not sound right.

* Inconsistent stories by or between both parents, changing stories.
   The facts of the incident change to fit the type of injuries.

Always check for any previous abuse of any children that die!

MUNCHAUSEN'S SYNDROME BY PROXY (MSBP)

Police death investigators must be able to adapt, develop, and use creative procedures when investigating child abuse. Infants are helpless victims in that they cannot adequately fight back and in most instances cannot verbally communicate the abuse. A form of child abuse, although not widely recognized, is a disorder known as Munchausen's Syndrome by Proxy (MSBP). MSBP is a form of long-term child abuse by a parent, usually the mother. The mortality rate for this type of abuse is high. A parent usually the mother, induces or reports physical symptoms in a child and fabricates a corresponding medical history that results in unnecessary medical evaluation and treatment. Involved parents may commit many deceptions. When the child is taken in for medical care, the parent will provide no apparent reason for the illness. The parent realizes that this will undoubtedly result in the hospitalization of the child for tests and observation. The child not only suffers from the actions of the parents, but are subjected to a battery of often unpleasant hospital tests.

Only the imagination of the parent limits the diversity of plausible symptoms. There are both mild and severe cases of MSBP. Some parents will go to great lengths to validate the reported symptoms of illness. In some cases the parent will even go so far as to inflict injury to the child. The syndrome may include apnea, seizures, hematuria, bleeding from the upper respiratory tract, vomiting, diarrhea, skin problems, vaginal and rectal bleeding, and cardiorespiratory arrests. Some cases of MSBP may induce seizures and non-accidental poisoning. Doctors and other medical staff need to be attentive to this type of abuse, especially when reoccurring illness goes unexplained.

MSBP perpetrators are found in all socioeconomic classes. The mother is the perpetrator in an alarming percentage of the incidents. The majority of the families in which MSBP occurs are dysfunctional, but tend to be intact. There may be a history of family problems. Mothers that facilitate abuse in this form may believe that the ill child will bring a closer relationship with the spouse. The mother may have feelings of insecurity, loneliness, or depression. Moreover, she may have had an emotionally deprived childhood with high probability of a history of physical abuse. MSBP may be a mechanism for expressing fear or anger. Perpetrators are seeking emotional support, love and nurturing.

Frequently, the mother has more than a basic medical knowledge that comes from previous experience in the health care profession. She may have a diagnosis of Munchausen Syndrome herself, a history of attempted suicide, and ongoing marital problems. The identification of perpetrators is crucial, because without treatment some mothers will continue and perhaps intensify their deceptions.

These cases usually start at infancy or at least by age two; however, the syndrome may take months or years to be diagnosed. The victims of abuse are generally children less that six years of age because older children are more likely to reveal the truth about their so-called symptoms. If MSBP continues as the child ages, the victim may even assist in the parent's deceptions. Although MSBP abusers will deny their actions while continuing the abuse, they may truly love the child.

Classifying MSBP is a difficult and sometimes lengthy process that involves the efforts of many people. The first step in identifying any case of child abuse is becoming aware and educated. The medical community and law enforcement must be knowledgeable about all aspects of MSBP. The life of a blameless infant depends on the commitment of the medical and judicial professionals. They must be quick to recognize, identify, and intervene in all types of child abuse. Law enforcement must make every effort to obtain the necessary evidence, not only to prosecute these individuals, but also to convict them. When abundant proof of abuse can be established, the police need to act quickly and efficiently. Quick action by law enforcement will prevent further child abuse to this child as well as any siblings.

CRIB DEATH

Note the position of the crib and the material that makes up the structure of the crib. Examine the crib for damage, paint chips, including the rail lift system, and any other defect. Measure the distance between the mattress and the side of the crib, the space between the rails, and the height between the mattress and the top of the rails in both the up and down position. Make measurements of distance from the floor to the mattress and the floor to the top of the rail in the up and the down position. Make note of the material makeup of the floor. The investigator should also make note of any objects inside the crib such as bedding, toys, bottles, pacifiers, or clothing. It should also be noted where any other siblings in the home might have been located during this time.

Chapter 16

SUICIDE

In Chapter 1 *Death Defined*, it was stated that any form of death can masquerade as another form. This is so factual in cases that could be suicide, but could also be a homicide or accidental death. It is not uncommon to have numerous cases that are reported as suicide, later changed to homicide after the death has been investigated. The cause of death may not always be what it appears to be, therefore, it is important to determine the correct cause and manner of death. If a case is ruled to be a suicide when in fact it is a homicide, justice is not served.

Men commit suicide twice as often as women. Suicides are a planned act that are usually done alone to prevent interruption. Most methods employed are swift and fatal. Guns are used most frequently. Suicide can occur in individuals at any age.

Attempted suicides are merely acts of impulsiveness. Twice as many females as males attempt suicide. The means used to facilitate suicide attempts are usually slow or totally ineffective. Provision is usually made to have the suicide interrupted either by prior notification or attempting suicide in the presence of another. In attempted suicides, the person has no real desire to die, and is merely looking for attention. Keep in mind that some attempted suicides are truly intended to be fatal but the attempt fails.

Several key factors can be used as indicators in regard to people contemplating suicide. Two common factors are related in the act of suicide. The first factor is depression. In many instances it may be reported to the police death investigator that the victim was not depressed. At that point several questions need to be resolved about previous behavior.

Questions About Depression

1. Depressed or gloomy for two weeks or more. Feeling of hope
   lessness.
2. Unable to sleep. May be severe.
3. Loss of appetite.
4. Loss of interest in life, sex or other hobbies or interests.
5. Personal hygiene.
6. Decrease of energy.
7. Slowed thinking or preoccupation.
8. Agitation, can't sit still.
9. Guilt. May or not be any factual basis.
10. Talk of death or suicide. Gloomy thoughts.

People can come out of depression with or without treatment.

Four or more of the aforementioned items place an individual into the depression category. I conducted a study of suicides using the ten factors of depression (see the end of this chapter). Most suicide victims were found to have at least four and as many as seven of the factors.

Alcoholism

The second factor is alcoholism. Suicide is a reaction to life. Usually about 90 percent of all alcoholics make known a suicidal intent. In either factor, depression or alcoholism, suicide seems like a logical choice.

1. Person drinks to excess.
2. Creates personal issues.
   a. Family
   b. Spouse, marital separation or divorce
   c. Police
   d. Health problems
   e. Job
   f. Financial
3. Cannot control drinking.

Figure 16.1. Suicide related to alcoholism. Victim had a long history of alcoholism and reported to the police his intention of committing suicide.

Teenage suicides have become increasingly common. Associated with suicide in teenagers is the phenomena of schoolmates committing suicide. Teen suicide may also take place if other family or friends have committed suicide. Teens that commit suicide fall under the category of being depressed. The teen victim may act upon impulse. Depression may be brought on by feelings of failure, a lost love interest, or other rejection, disciplinary problems, or an embarrassment.

Suicides that take place while in police custody is of major concern. Whenever an individual is set on taking his or her own life, it is not always easy to intercept that desire. This person does not always convey his or her intent to the police, therefore, the subject is placed in the normal inmate environment to be left with their own imagination.

Many correctional facilities today allow for a segregated area of lock-up to protect candidates of suicide. These safe areas are only good if police are aware of the potential of suicide.

In some instances, a police officer dispatched to a suicide or an attempted suicide is expected to play several important roles regarding this specific type of call. In situations where the police are called to prevent a suicide, they themselves are subject to serious injury by the subject. The police officer may have to actually respond and rescue, provide first aid, or call for medical assistance. The officer may also be required to notify family, make arrangements for children who are present, or follow up with mental health for commitment.

In suicide or attempted suicide investigations, you must preserve the scene and evidence. In situations where the person is still alive and has been transported to the hospital, any evidence of poisons, drugs or prescriptions found should be **immediately** taken to the hospital. Suicides do occur and there are reasons why people took their own life. The death investigator must determine that the death was a suicide and the reason why it occurred. It is just as important to remember that just because the case was reported as a suicide, does not mean that it actually happened.

Case History 1

In April 1984, a male telephoned police to say that his girlfriend had shot herself in the head. The case was first thought to be suicide. The boyfriend gave his story stating that he was in the living room when he heard a gun shot. Upon entering the bedroom he found that his girlfriend had shot herself once in the head. The entire bedroom was processed for physical evidence. In fact, the entire bedroom from ceiling to floor was dismantled and reassembled at the crime lab. No evidence was initially developed to disprove suicide. Although the boyfriend tried to be convincing, he tried to be too convincing. During the next year enough evidence was obtained to get a charge of murder and conviction.

Note: A large percentage of suicides are committed by gunshot wound. Most suicides with a handgun are done at contact range. As pointed out in Chapter 10 *Gunshot Wounds*, these types of wounds can cause severe bruising, especially around the eyes in head injuries. This is not evidence that the victim was beaten and then shot.

Suicides can be difficult investigations to work simply because of the personal feelings of family members regarding the victim. No family member wants to believe their loved one took their own life. Families will go to great lengths to cover up the suicide of a loved one or to argue that the death was a homicide. Exercise caution when dealing with the family. The first contact with the suicide victim's family usually produces the best opportunity to obtain valuable information relating to the victim's condition before death. Stories may change after the initial shock of hearing a family member committed suicide.

Study

During a ten-year period from 1984 to 1994, I requested that all detectives, and crime scene officers of the Sangamon County Sheriff's Department conduct a survey with family and friends of suicide victims. This survey contained questions concerning the victim's demeanor over the last 30 days of their life. The study asked questions relating to depression, insomnia, personal appearance and hygiene, paranoia, personal conduct, and changes in attitude. All information was then placed into the detective bureau's main computer by a division secretary in a formatted field. The file format allowed for the retrieval of information by each of the ten personal behavior items listed under depression in this chapter. The findings were then established from the information of those cases submitted over this ten-year period.

Findings

One hundred suicide cases were reviewed for the ten-year period, 50 were men and 50 were women. In 90 cases, at least four of the ten behavior changes were noted, with ten cases having a notable margin of error in collecting the pertinent data. No significance was noted by gender. Of those 90 cases that contained at least four of the behavior changes, 60, or two-thirds, of the suicides had seven or more of the changes noted in their behavior prior to death.

Chapter 17

HOMICIDE

ALL HOMICIDE INVESTIGATIONS are important, however, there will be some cases that mean more to the death investigator than others. It is just human nature that you will be more affected by one case over all others. There is something that makes a particular case just a little more significant than any other. As for me I can remember the pertinent facts of every case. My family thinks it's strange that I associate events in my life by the dates of murder cases. In my career I had murder victims that were from every walk of life, the wife, the son, the parent, the rich entrepreneur, the lady of the evening, the drug dealer, or the husband whose wife contracted a retired state trooper to murder him.

Like everyone that has worked in death investigation, there was one homicide that was more significant than other cases. In fact, it was the most significant case I was ever to work. The reason that it is mentioned in this handbook is for the numerous investigative techniques that were employed during the course of the investigation. In 1974, Sangamon County Sheriff's Deputy William D. Simmons was found shot to death in his patrol car in an isolated rural area of the county just outside Springfield, Illinois. The case went unsolved for nearly 20 years before an arrest and conviction were obtained.

The scene had been searched for any type of evidence. We found one fingerprint that apparently was unrelated on a beer can several yards away. Two bullets were recovered from the autopsy that were used for ballistic comparison. Several weapons were submitted for comparisons, with no match. Not much else in the way of any type of evidence was found. However, other techniques used in the investigation were polygraph deception, interviews with sodium pentothal, psychics, hypnosis, scene reconstruction, informants and even offers for a reward. The only reason the case was ever solved was due to the dedication and hard work of the men and women of the Sangamon County Sheriff's Department.

The field of death investigation is something you must give serious consideration to before making this area your chosen field of duty. Do not be fooled by the thought and misconception that being a homicide detective is a glorious job. This particular aspect of law enforcement will demand great sacrifice and dedication. It can consume a great deal of your personal, or family life. The homicide detective cannot help but take their cases home. If he or she is not careful, the case can consume them if they lose sight of the fact their family must come first. On the other hand, homicide investigation can be the most rewarding career endeavor that anyone in police work can ever undertake. It will take more than just a casual interest; commitment and devotion are mandatory. Through the media and the eyes of the public, the homicide unit of any law enforcement agency will be highly scrutinized by its ability to solve murders. Moreover, although this country has liberalized its way of thinking, homicide is still taken seriously by the general population.

There are a great many unsolved homicides throughout the country, however, the investigation of homicide is not as complex as one might think. Continuity of ideals and principals of homicide investigations are paramount. Obviously, some murder cases will mandate substantially more investigative effort than another. Every homicide investigation needs to be worked with a methodical approach from start to finish.

The police death investigator needs to acquire some basic understanding of murder investigations in general. You need to have a complete knowledge and understanding of the laws governing your investigation. The police death investigator needs to stay on top of the rules of evidence, as well as new or improved investigative techniques. Most, if not all, of the update, knowledge and skills can be attained by reading new reference material or by continuing education through in-service training or college courses. All too often, the homicide detective can become wrapped up in his or her caseload and cannot find the time to expand or to improve abilities.

As was stated in Chapter 2, *The Role Of The Death Investigator*, ultimately the burden of investigating a murder falls upon the police death investigator. The coroner, medical examiner, and the pathologist do not investigate deaths. Their help and assistance may prove to be invaluable in the investigation; however, it is up to the death investigator to solve the case. Being a homicide detective comes with a heavy weight of responsibility not every police officer can fulfill. The job is more than just gathering the facts, linking evidence, or conducting interviews. It requires seeing that someone who unjustly took another person's life does not get away with it.

Obviously, the first important aspect is safe arrival to the crime scene. The investigator should enter the scene by the route least likely to disturb evidence. Be sure and note your route of entry. **Make sure the scene is safe**. Even if other officers are at the scene, ensure the scene is secure before starting your necessary tasks. Always check the victim for any signs of life that might be present. Touch the victim to check for a pulse and for the warmth or coolness of the body.

If the victim is living, medical assistance should be summoned if they have not been called. Consider taking a dying declaration from the victim if they are conscious. Be familiar with the law in your jurisdiction concerning a dying declaration. A dying declaration can be accepted as competent evidence and an exception to the hearsay rule. The acceptance of the dying declaration is based on the fact the victim knew and understood that he or she was dying and if death does occur. Attempt to ascertain the name of the person who did the violence. If the name of the assailant is not known by the victim, then obtain as much of an identification by description as possible: sex, race, height, weight, hair and eye color, type of clothing, and/or type of vehicle used.

If the victim is unconscious at the time of your arrival, assign an officer to remain with the victim at all times. This includes transport to the hospital and whatever treatment proceedings the hospital will allow, in the event a dying declaration can be taken. The hospital will relax most restrictions if they are aware that the officer is present for the purpose of obtaining a dying declaration from the victim should they regain consciousness. You must make it clear to the hospital staff the importance of your attempt to obtain the declaration.

If possible, photograph the victim before he or she is removed from the scene. Use the Polaroid and get as many scene photos as possible before the live victim needs to be transported. If time and conditions do not allow for taking photos before the victim's removal, carefully note and sketch the position immediately while still fresh in your mind. The tried and true chalk outline works well when the victim needs to be transported.

It is important to obtain physical evidence from the victim. The police officer that accompanies the victim to the hospital should collect and mark the victim's clothing as they become available. Although most hospitals are aware of the significance of physical evidence and the gathering of the clothes are left to them, the medical staff could inadvertently contaminate the clothing. Hospital staff might place all the clothing in the same bag, which might contaminate or even destroy evidence.

The scene should be roped off or *secured* in such a way to prevent unnecessary or unauthorized persons from entering the scene. Prevent anyone from touching the body or disturbing anything. When handling an outdoor scene security becomes even more of a problem. Crowds will gather and they cannot only complicate your investigation by their presence, but can also become enraged and be out of control. Be sure you have sufficient support. Additionally, the media has photographic or filming equipment that can produce high quality images from a great distance. You do not want your entire crime scene investigation on the evening news.

Once the scene is secured, there is no need to rush the actual investigation. Evidence that must be immediately collected must be gathered first. Take the time to hold a brief preinvestigation conference. This conference should include the coroner, medical examiner or pathologist, and all detectives that will be involved with any part of the investigation. This conference will afford an opportunity for all participants involved with the investigation to have their respective duties outlined before starting. This time can also be utilized to bring forth information known at this point.

Scene photography should include photographs of the entrance and exit routes to the scene. You cannot take too many pictures. Additionally, include all possible locations that are related to the scene. It is important that all rooms at a house scene be photographed. Something may have happened in an adjoining room that will be of crucial significance as the investigation continues. Photograph all items of evidence, footprints, spent shells or casings, weapons, blood, etc., in the crime scene. Outdoor scenes should include photos of streets and intersections. If possible, higher overhead pictures should be taken. These can be useful in considering a full and accurate depiction of the scene. Photographs taken of the victim at the scene need to include Polaroids that are taken immediately upon discovery of the body. Other photos should include the victim, clothing, blood, powder residue and other substances. These photographs should include full length and closeups of pertinent items in the scene.

Be sure to make careful notes regarding the position the body is in, the relationship to other objects in the scene, the position and the condition of the clothing, identification, and location of substances on the body or clothing. It is also necessary to note any alteration of deceased's position before your arrival, as determined from witnesses or other police officers. The police death investigator should conduct a scene survey before attempting a crime scene search. This scene survey is similar to the preinvestigation conference. All police death investigators should discuss the potential of evidence with the ID technician. Take a few moments to consider the type of homicide, then consider items of evidence that should be related to this type of murder. This will assist you in locating evidence linked to the crime. Even more importantly, this methodical approach may indicate that the evidence does not fit the crime. Since one type of death can masquerade as another, recovered evidence should link to the suspected cause of the homicide.

As previously discussed, whenever possible the death investigator should attend the autopsy of the victim. The coroner or the medical examiner will make arrangements for the body to be transported to the morgue. The body of the deceased and the items or substances found on it or contained within it are evidence for which you are responsible. For this reason a police officer should accompany the victim's body to the morgue. As with any investigation the chain of custody is important so that any evidence recovered can be admitted in court.

At the postmortem examination several items of evidence need to be collected. In any major case autopsy, evidentiary items such as fingerprints, fingernail scrapings, palmprints, and blood samples need to be analyzed. Hair samples should also be collected. These hair samples should include head, facial, body, and pubic hair.

Collect and preserve each item of physical evidence obtained by the pathologist. Place each item separately in an individual paper bag or container. Do not allow clothing collected from the victim to come in contact with each other. All items of clothing must be bagged separately. The location on a particular garment of bloodstains, hair or other substances may be critical. The pathologist will mark x-rays of corresponding numbers of bullets or the foreign materials such as glass or knife fragments that have been removed from the body. It is the responsibility of the pathologist to examine the contents of the stomach. The digestive process of food eaten before death might provide some range of time that death occurred.

Some pathology departments are very proficient in taking necessary autopsy photographs. Some smaller operations, or those with limited budgets, might not take a sufficient amount of pictures during the autopsy. If this is the case, the police need to take an adequate amount of photographs in conjunction with the department of pathology. However, it is of utmost importance that police are careful not to have their photographs entered into evidence as pictures from the autopsy if the pathologist has photos from which he or she intends to testify.

It is the role of the homicide detective to organize and control the investigation. He or she must also be mindful of the responsibility to provide investigative updates to chain of command supervisors, other investigators and prosecutors. Other duties include the establishment of a major casebook. This casebook should contain an index of contents, initial reports, follow-up reports, evidence reports, medical reports, witness statements, background on deceased and scene notes, sketches and photographs. If applicable, information relating to a defendant, including any statements or background on the defendant, should be contained in the book.

Copies of the major casebook must be updated on a regular basis, at least once a day during an active, ongoing murder investigation. Copies of the casebook should be provided to all principal detectives and the prosecutor assigned to the case. If necessary, copies should be distributed to other agencies that may be assisting in the investigation. In some instances periodic briefings to outside assisting agencies may suffice.

Since all death investigations are worked as a homicide until the case can be shown to be a suicide, accident or natural death, the method of approach to the death investigation should always be the same. The obvious difference is that in the murder case the person or persons responsible for taking another's life should be sought. While developing a suspect profile to the crime, keep in mind there could be multiple suspects. The suspect(s) can be any sex and be from early to very old in age.

When the suspect is located at the scene of the crime, certain investigative functions must be done immediately. The suspect needs to be advised of Miranda, the constitutional rights afforded to all suspects. If any questions are asked, then Miranda warnings must be issued to the suspect. All too often police officers have a fear of providing Miranda. The fear is that the suspect will ask for an attorney and not say anything. There are ways to provide Miranda warnings and still not have the suspect request an attorney. The technique of providing Miranda warnings should be practiced frequently, it will be used more than your firearm.

While there are numerous schools that provide excellent training in interviews and interrogations, there are a few simple rules that need to be followed. If the interview is a custodial interview, then Miranda must be given. The word *custodial* can be misleading. Perhaps a much simpler way to understand if Miranda is to be given is to always give Miranda. This is especially true if you intend taking the person into custody and if the person says anything incriminating, they will be placed into custody. The furnishing of Miranda should be done by reading Miranda. Any police officer can commit Miranda to memory, but may have trouble recalling the words while testifying just how they gave a suspect their Miranda rights. Read the card during the interview. Read the card in court.

Occasionally the suspect, while at the scene, will offer to reenact how the crime took place. This is obviously very beneficial to your investigation. Your scene investigation, crime scene search, and evidence collection should be completed prior to reenactment. Be sure that any evidence contained in or on the suspect is noted and recovered before having them enter the scene. A sharp defense attorney might attempt to show the defendant had evidence on them from this reenactment and just as important, videotape the suspect's reenactment.

Once the suspect has been developed, you need to conduct a complete investigation on that person. The death investigator needs to determine the suspect's flight from the scene. By what route did the suspect leave and what, if any, was the mode of transportation? If a vehicle was used, it should be processed for physical evidence. Determine what clothing the suspect was wearing at the time of the murder and carefully collect and preserve the clothing for evidentiary purposes.

The suspect should be photographed. Take pictures of the suspect fully clothed to establish condition, color of clothing, and the suspect's physical appearance. Photographed unclothed as soon as possible after arrest to establish any evidence of the suspect's physical condition. Obtain closeups of any injuries such as scrapes, cuts, or bruises. Approximately 12 hours after these initial photographs, take additional photographs of the suspect unclothed to determine any changes in the suspect's physical appearance. Even if the suspect has no obvious injuries the photographs should be taken. The suspect may claim to have received injuries from the victim or the police. Photographs showing an absence of any injury might be of value.

Most homicides that occur indicate that the victim and the suspect were acquainted in some way. Those types of killings can be divided into four categories:

Spouse Killing: Husband kills wife or wife kills husband.
Parent Killing: Parent kills child or child kills parent.
Altercation: Quarrel among other relatives or friends.
Romantic Triangle: Lover's quarrel.

Reasons for murder often lead the investigator towards a suspect. Cause for murder can occur while drinking; during drug deals or during the commission of a crime such as burglary, robbery or sexual assault; and in some cases for revenge towards the victim. Take a methodical approach to survey the reason for the murder. That survey can provide valuable leads in the development of a suspect.

SERIAL MURDERS

There are, of course, instances where the victim and suspect had no prior knowledge of one another. One specific form concerning this type of murder is serial murder. It is important to remember that two categories of serial murders can be referred to as those in an isolated geographic location such as a particular city, and the other being the serial murders that occur across different parts of the country as in the southwest or northeast United States. Serial murders in a major city have a better likelihood of being investigated by one police agency even though it may involve several different divisions of that agency.

In the across the country serial murder, many different agencies may be involved and they have less chance of realizing their case is just one of several in a geographic region. These types of murders can go undetected for long periods of time and have a large number of victims.

Serial murderers have captivated the communities of our country by their heinous deeds. Such killers are people like The Clown John Wayne Gacy, Son of Sam David Berkowitz, Night Stalker Richard Ramirez, Boston Strangler Albert Desalvo, Henry Lee Lucas, Richard Speck, Wayne Williams, Ted Bundy, Jeffery Dahmer and, of course, Charles Manson. While some serial killers never left their neighborhood, others were known to have traveled across several states.

It is imperative that all police agencies communicate. It has been a long-standing tradition that law enforcement agencies do not talk to one another. This in itself has been a strong reason why serial murders can have significant numbers of homicide victims. The implementation of VICAP has helped.

VICAP, initially conceived by Detective Pierce Brooks of the LAPD, acts as a clearinghouse for case information, collecting homicide, and assault information from across the country. VICAP can reduce informational gaps between the thousands of policing agencies in the United States. The 1980s launched law enforcement into the computer age. By 1985 the Federal Bureau of Investigation had begun VICAP programs. VICAP has been handcuffed only by the lack of data submitted from death investigators throughout the United States. It takes teamwork, like most databases they are only as valuable as the amount of information entered.

SEXUAL HOMICIDE

Sex-related crimes raise a greater variety of problems than any other one aspect of criminal investigation. Some sex crimes have offenses which, in the minds of most ordinary people, have no relationship to sex whatsoever. Realistically, police involvement is based on two elements; namely, invasion of the rights of the victim, and deviation from the normal community standards. Keep in mind that some community standards in one geographical location may not shock the standards of a community in another location.

The majority of all sexual offenses are serious in nature to the police. However, some offenses are regarded to be more significant or at a higher threat level. Unfortunately, often is the case where the minor sex offense is escalated as the offender becomes more active. The victim of a minor sex-related crime, such as window peeping, may not be harmed physically. Despite the lack of physical harm, the victim may suffer from mental injury. Additionally, the offender may interpret a minor sex offense that has gone unpunished as an open invitation to continue or intensify his or her actions.

Offenders who seek deviant sexual satisfaction may often attempt to find stronger forms of stimulation. The person may practice a mild or even inoffensive type of self sexual gratification only to have the need for greater thrills grow stronger. These thrills can be of a sexual nature or can be a need to increase a risk factor of getting caught.

Once an individual begins to escalate his or her sexual practices beyond what is acceptable by community morals, he or she may also lose the ability to stop. Once the capability to cross the moral and legal lines is achieved, the person can and will continue until he or she commits major crimes. Most mass murders are said to fall in this category. Moreover, just the opposite may also occur. A person who has never committed any type of crime in his or her life may, without announcement, commit a serious sex crime. It is not always easy to understand what motivates an individual to commit a sexual offense. It may be easier to comprehend that motives for this type of behavior can be classified by type.

1. The offense is a substitute for normal sexual activity.
2. The offense offers a variety to normal sexual activity.
3. The offense provides an excitement that would otherwise prevent the subject from performing sexually.
4. The offense heightens the level of sexual activity.
5. The offense provides complete sexual gratification.
6. The offense is committed just because it is wrong to do so.

As mentioned in Chapter 6, hanging is a form of asphyxia. Hanging is performed by some individuals to heighten sexual stimulation. The reduced supply of blood and oxygen to the brain produces a hypoxia or a hallucination. Often is the case where the victim is unable to release themselves, resulting in death. Other sexual activity may include the giving or receiving of pain. The desire to be hurt is called masochism. A desire to hurt another person is called sadism. In extreme cases, the sadist may have the desire to inflict actual wounds to the victim. This urge can elevate to the cutting or stabbing of the victim. Piquerism is the designation given or associated when the victim is murdered and then the body is mutilated. Some persons can become overly sexually excited by the sight of fresh blood which is referred to as vampirism. In these instances, the offender will drink the blood of his or her victim. Still another form of deviance called cannibalism is when the offender has a craving for human flesh. This has no spiritual or religious value, simply a source of food.

There are some practical tips that the death investigator can follow during the homicide investigation. Call upon other experienced investigators to assist or give advice. Be careful in questioning witnesses, they may turn out to be principals in the crime. Do not divulge critical information carelessly to the public, witnesses, or the media. Separate all witnesses prior to interviews and keep in mind that only one opportunity to interview a particular witness may be possible.

Most of all, remember homicide investigation takes **TEAMWORK**!

HOMICIDE STATISTICS

During the 20 years that I spent as a death investigator with the Sangamon County Sheriff's Department in Springfield, Illinois, I had the opportunity to research several areas of death investigation. Studies were conducted from analyzing cases related to suicide, excited delirium, and homicide. One such study was to examine information developed from our homicide investigations. Sangamon County, with Springfield as its county seat and the capitol city of Illinois, is located 180 miles south of Chicago and approximately 90 miles north of St. Louis, Missouri. Interstate 55 connects it to both major cities. During this time period Sangamon County had a population of just over 200,000 people. It could be said that Sangamon County typified rural America.

The following statistical information was gathered over a 20-year period from 1974 to 1994.

Victims by gender:
    63% male victims   37% female victims

Assailants by gender:
    90% male assailants   10% female assailants

Victims by race:
94% caucasian victims   6% other victims

Assailant by race:
80% caucasian assailant   20% other assailant

Victim/Assailant relationship:
66% of all homicide victims knew their assailants

Mechanism used in homicide:
Gunshot *	53%
Cutting or stabbing	32%
Club	6%
Vehicle	6%
Strangulation	2%
Drowning	1%

Gunshot:*
Handgun	85%
Rifle	15%
Shotgun	5%

HOMICIDE CHECKLIST

Crime Scene

1. Your first responsibility is to arrive safely.
2. If life exists, provide first aid and have victim transported to the hospital.
3. Identify the location and area where the victim was found.
4. Preserve the scene, do not touch or remove anything until it has been noted, recorded, and photographed.
5. Make observation and notes.
6. Take photographs, Polaroids, 35 mm and video.
7. Take all necessary measurements.
8. Make your crime scene sketch.
9. Collection of physical evidence.

Victim

1. Note location, position, and condition of the body.
2. Check for any after-death changes.
3. Note the environmental temperature where the body is located.
4. Note the type, and location of wounds.
5. Note how the victim is dressed.
6. Make note of any blood on the victim, on the clothes, or located anywhere around the victim.
7. Wrap the victim in a white sheet and place in a body bag.
8. Positively identify the body as soon as possible.

Witnesses

1. Separate and isolate if possible.
2. Take individual statements rather than a group statement.
3. Obtain all pertinent information that identifies the witness.

Chapter 18

THE SCENE

THE INVESTIGATION OF DEATH is a teamwork endeavor and involves all components of the law enforcement system. Various aspects of the scene and scene observations are important from a medical-legal standpoint. The information gathered at the scene must have proper documentation to preserve this information so that it is accepted by our courts. From the time the incident occurs, the scene continues to change. The scene can change on its own. The body will deteriorate as time progresses. The scene will also change by the result of necessary responders such as police officers, investigators and medical personnel. It is important to realize that it is possible to have multiple scenes.

Each crime scene needs to have determined boundaries. If manpower is available, three separate perimeters should be established. The first perimeter is established by the uniform division and serves as the first boundary. This boundary controls the public onlookers and the media. This perimeter must be established at a distance, and the innermost perimeter where evidence will be collected should not be viewed from this first boundary.

The second boundary can be defined as the staging area of the crime scene. Only the necessary and authorized personnel should be within this secondary perimeter. Authorized personnel will be emergency medical personnel, police officers, crime scene technicians, death investigators, and the coroner or the pathologist. This area needs to be secured and must not be an area where physical evidence could be collected. If evidence recovery in this area is a possibility, then the area must be searched before using it to stage the crime scene investigation.

After discussing which methodical approach will be utilized to search and collect items of evidence from the crime scene, the third and final boundary can be determined. This third perimeter is what can be established as the crime scene where the actual crime was committed. Inside this perimeter the search for evidence, collection of evidence, and all necessary photographs will be taken. Remember that some crimes can have one or more crime scenes and each crime scene may be as small as a room or as big as a football field.

Proper documentation should include Polaroids, 35mm stills, video, notes and sketches. Documentation of the scene through photography and sketches help clarify written reports and provide a permanent record. Establishing a common and accurate understanding of a particular setting or crime scene is eased when testimony is accompanied with photos and crime scene sketches.

Polaroid

Use a Polaroid in all death investigation cases. Several Polaroids should be taken as soon as possible of the victim at the scene. The police death investigator can take the Polaroids, he or she does not need to be an expert. Always take the Polaroids to the autopsy; pathologists appreciate the opportunity to see what the body looked like in the scene.

35mm Stills

These photographs are for admission in court if needed, and should be taken by a photographer experienced in shooting pictures at a crime scene. In order for the photographs to be admissible they must not be inflammatory and must be free of distortion or misrepresentation. The photographer must be able to testify to the validity of the photo.

Video

Video should not be used as a substitute for 35 mm and should be taken at each scene. The video should include the approach into the scene, the interior, the body and the flight of any perpetrator. Different departments may have established guidelines concerning whether the video should be narrated or not.

Notes

Notes are useful for preparing reports and preparation for court. Notes are subject to review by the courts. Notes can assist in recalling places, events, incidents, and other pertinent facts from the scene. Notes will help detail information obtained from witnesses, victims, or suspects. Notes should not be edited or erased.

Sketches

Photographs and videos do not always give the viewer exact distance and sizes of objects or their true relationships. Sketches can supplement both notes and photography. Sketches will provide accurate measurements of pertinent items such as bodies and weapons. Sketches are subject to review by the court.

Observations

1. The exact position and location of the body when first seen.
2. Objects in contact with the body and location of these contacts.
3. Any alterations of the body position and its location after first observed.
4. Rigidity; present, absent or inappropriate.
5. Lividity; present, absent, location, fixed or non-fixed, inappropriate.
6. Environmental temperature.
7. General condition of clothing when first seen; intact, disarray, open, blood, foreign material, defects. Any alteration of clothing after first observed.
8. Items of clothing which might be normally on the body.
9. Characteristics of blood on the body; smears, direction of streaks. Were these characteristics altered by change in body position?

Handling the Body at the Scene

The handling of the body at the scene and transport is a vital aspect of the death investigation. The hands and the feet often have important evidence and this evidence can be lost by careless handling of the body. As soon as it is appropriate at the scene, the hands and the feet must be bagged with paper sacks and appropriately fixed to the forearms and legs with tape. Plastic bags must not be used. Do not cover the body; especially covering and then uncovering of the victim. The body of a deceased victim should not be covered until thoroughly processed for evidence. Wrap the body in a white sheet and place the victim in a body bag to be transported. For purpose of the chain of custody of evidence, a police office should accompany the body from the scene until it is released to the coroner's office or morgue.

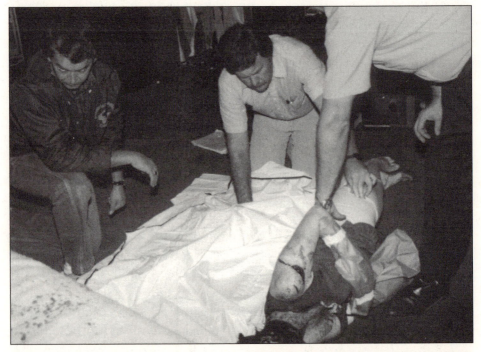

Figure 18.1. Preparing the homicide victim for transport to the morgue. The victim is placed on a white sheet and the hands are bagged to preserve any evidence that might be found.

There may be reasons to process or examine the body before it is transported to the morgue. The on-scene pathologist may want to examine the victim for stages of rigor mortis, livor mortis or decomposition, position of the body, condition of the clothing, or wounds. These observations can be helpful in establishing time of death or the cause and manner of death. Such preliminary inquiries may provide pertinent information to help the police investigation progress in a more timely manner. Extra care must be taken in the course of any preliminary examination of the body so as not to disturb or contaminate evidence that may not yet be collected.

Personnel

Those persons present within the immediate area of the crime scene should be only those needed to assist in the investigation, scene processing, or removal of the victim. It may become necessary to request other officials present to refrain from examining or disturbing objects or aspect of the scene. You may have to ask or suggest that those unnecessary personnel vacate the scene.

Release of the Scene

One of the last duties of the death investigator is to release the scene. Obviously, the scene should not be released until all examination, processing and collection of evidence has been completed. The release should be effected at the earliest practicable time, particularly in instances where public activity has been suspended. It is important to realize that once a scene has been released, it may be necessary to obtain a search warrant to regain entry. However, return trips may find evidence has been contaminated or has disappeared altogether.

Information from the Scene

Information should be obtained from the individuals first arriving on the scene, the uniformed police officers, firemen or paramedics. What was the position of the body? Document the precise procedures of first responders, CPR, removing or cutting of clothing. Note any movement of a weapon or the movement of other objects that may have been in contact with the body.

OUTSIDE SCENE

Precise description of the immediate surrounding environment, terrain, vegetation and expected animals in the area should be noted. Document the general meteorological conditions, such as rain, snow or electrical storms. Provide descriptions for access points to the body and visibility of the body from paths or roads. Determine if the environmental evidence relates to how the body arrived at the sight when found. Evidence that might be present would be drag marks or blood trails. Check for environmental evidence such as a weapon or blood that indicates death occurred at the scene where the body was found .

Figure 18.2. The outdoor scene investigation can occur in all types of weather. The extremely hot or the brutally cold temperatures can understandably hinder your investigative efforts.

INSIDE SCENE

Give a prescise description of the immediate surrounding environment. Note local temperature in the immediate region of the body and the overall room temperature. Note any evidence of pets or pests that might be present in the structure. Document the surroundings. Are they tidy, untidy or is there inappropriate disarray?

BODIES FOUND IN VEHICLES

In instances where bodies are found in vehicles, several items should be checked and documented. Determine if the ignition switch is "on" or "off." Check the contents of the gas tank for volume. Check the heater/air conditioner and radio to see if they are in the "on" or "off" position. Check for the presence of engine heat or evidence of exhaust fumes.

BODIES FOUND IN WATER

Bodies found in water, fully immersed or floating, present several challenges for the death investigation team. Since each recovery is different, every retrieval effort will be different. Once again, your preplanning is important. Determine the best way to approach a particular situation, keeping in mind the preservation of evidence that may still be on the body. Bodies, although in water, have potential for the finding of some types of valuable evidence. Trace evidence, such as hairs and fibers, may still be recovered. In some instances, after years in water, some evidentiary samples can be found. Trace evidence may be found in the teeth, fingernails, toenails, vagina and anal cavity. The head hair and pubic hair of the victim may hold the best conceivable location for collecting evidence.

Give a general description of the area including currents, bank characteristics, bottom characteristics, water temperature, and expected aquatic or marine animals. Document all methods for removal of the body, including information relating to the site of removal of the body. If possible, describe the location of entry of the body into the water. Note any resuscitative attempts and watercraft usage in the area. Provide general meteorological conditions such as rain, ice or electrical storms. Take a water sample.

ASPECTS COMMON TO ALL LOCATIONS

Description including location of blood, vomit, seminal ejaculate, feces and other body materials found in the area of the body are necessary. Determination if origin of these types of items are from the victim or the assailant also needs to be established. Also note any drug paraphernalia, drugs or poisons in the area. Document the recovery of any weapons.

SEXUAL PRACTICES

Items found in the scene which may relate to unusual sexual practices should be documented and placed into evidence. Items such as pornographic literature, neck ligatures, ropes or cords, other devices used for bondage and penis substitutes should be photographed and taken into evidence. Check for any improperly operating electrical apparatus that could be located in the scene.

PROCEDURES RELATIVE TO THE BODY

Give an exact description and position of the body and the relationship to all surrounding objects and structures. Describe the location, appearance and amount of streaks or splotches of blood, vomit, seminal ejaculate, feces or other body materials on the body, the victim's clothing, and in the surrounding environment. Describe all items of clothing including how clothing is attached to the body and any defects in the clothing. Identify all items attached to the body which are clearly visible at the scene such as eyeglasses, ornamental jewelry, watches or hearing aids. Provide an exact position and location of all items which may have been previously attached to the body but which are now detached. This could include such items as headgear, eye-glasses, gloves, dentures or ornamental jewelry. **SUBMIT WITH THE BODY**.

BURIED BODIES

Excavation

We can categorize two forms of buried bodies. The first form is the intentional and unlawful disposal of a body to assist in preventing the detection of a crime. For the intent and purpose of this section, a buried body will be illustrated by any of the following: the victim is placed into a shallow mound, or hidden under all forms of debris, dumped along a roadway, or placed in a field or wooded area. This location is often labeled the decomposition site and does not necessarily mean that the body was actually placed into a grave. This decomposition site is most likely where trace evidence can best be found in this type of investigation.

The site should be examined for the presence of any marks in the soil that may indicate how the body arrived to this area. If the body was carried, there may be marks left by the person(s) who disposed of the victim. If the victim was not carried, then tire marks or drag marks might be observed. You will also want to check for the presence of animal tracks. Animals may have been drawn to the site by odor and may dig into the decomposition site to scavenge the remains. If this does occur, animals may drag parts of the body to other locations.

Obviously, the body has a better chance to be observed if it is simply dumped and not covered or placed in a shallow mound. However, the police death investigator has some signs that he or she can look for that will help locate the decomposing corpse. Body fluids that leak from the body during decomposition may stain the surrounding soil. The soil can become acidic and prevent growth of vegetation. Due to ammonia released from the corpse, other vegetation, like leaves on low overhanging branches, can turn yellow or brown. There may also be visible signs of insect activity in the decomposition site.

Figure 18.3. A body in a casket found in the basement of a home. Exhumation from a grave site had to be considered. Additionally, it had to be contemplated if the body was hidden in an attempt to hide a death.

Procedures for the Buried Body

1. Take photographs, including the decomposition site and the surroundings. If possible, take higher elevation photos from above the burial location.
2. Cautiously remove vegetation, twigs, or sticks or other brush from around the decomposition site. Carefully examine each item removed for trace evidence.
3. With the use of a metal detector, mindful not to disturb the soil, sweep the area to determine if any metallic objects lay beneath the soil.
4. Any area that indicated a metallic object should be meticulously excavated, immediately sifting through each particle of dirt.

5. Excavation of the decomposition site is better determined by the type of excavation at each site. As each circumstance will be different, several removal techniques should be considered and fully discussed before any digging begins.
    a. Dig another grave site, adjacent to the grave the victim is in, making access to the body from the side, is one consideration.
    b. Dig a trench completely around the grave site, and then remove layers of soil from above the corpse, going down from the top.
    c. Any method of approach that works in a given situation.
6. Choose a method that works best, one that helps keep the integrity of your dig and preserves the evidence. Be sure to sift all soil as it is removed.
7. Once the body is removed, be sure to run the metal detector over the area where the body lay.
8. It may be an advantage to dig a foot or more beneath the area where the body lay to search for evidence. This soil should be sifted. Be observant of finding pertinent evidence.

The detailed decomposition site processing can assist the police death investigator with the determination of the cause and manner of death, a range for time of death, or perhaps even more significantly, an identification of the victim.

Exhumation

The second form of a buried body is defined as the intentional and legal disposal of a body, more commonly understood as a funeral procedure. In certain circumstances, it may be necessary to legally remove a previously buried body. This removal of a buried corpse is known as exhumation. Although the removal process of the legally buried corpse may be similar to that outlined in excavation, the proper term for legally removing a buried body is to "exhume" the body.

There are several reasons that may be necessary to exhume a body. The body may be exhumed if there is significant information to indicate that the buried corpse was improperly identified. An exhumation may be performed to prove a crime was committed. For example, the victim may have been poisoned by another person and buried before the homicide could be discovered. Another reason for exhumation would be to collect evidence that was not obtained before burial. Lastly, the body may be exhumed to change interment locations.

An exhumation requires an order signed by a judge, and then only after a strong argument for cause is presented. This order will need to grant authority to disinter, remove, and reinter the corpse. The exhumation may also call for special permits from state and county agencies. Some states may request for a waiver for exhumation signed by the family. For several reasons the court-ordered exhumation may be the more prudent avenue to obtain permission.

The police death investigator, the prosecutor, and the pathologist or medical examiner have certain things to consider prior to exhumation. If a previous postmortem examination was performed, what were the findings of that autopsy? Additionally, if an autopsy was done, where are the organs? Also to be considered, was the body embalmed? These are all relevant questions that need to be carefully considered before the exhumation operation begins.

Procedures for Exhumation

1. Identify and verify the exact grave site, before exhumation begins.
2. Photograph the headstone or the grave marker.
3. Determine if the vault is concrete and if the casket is wood or metal.
4. Photograph or video the exhumation process.
5. Take soil samples from around the casket.
6. Take fluid samples from the casket.
7. Let the pathologist or medical examiner do their job.
8. Consider toxicology, despite the corpse having been embalmed.

TRANSPORTATION OF THE BODY

Transport the body in the position which it was found. The body should be accompanied to the morgue by a police officer. If the body cannot be accompanied by a police officer, place the body in a body bag sealed with evidence tape. Include with the body all items that may have been removed from the pockets and examined. As stated previously, submit with the body all objects and clothing which may have been previously attached. Be careful not to contaminate any evidence. **DON'T FORGET THE WEAPON**. Handle the body carefully with minimal disturbance and with the least disturbance to the clothes. Handle the hands and feet with extreme caution and bag the hands and feet with paper sacks as soon as possible, thus preserving any evidence that might be present.

QUESTIONS THAT NEED TO BE ANSWERED

Is the area in which the body was found the actual scene where death occurred? Consider if the fatal injuries occured elsewhere, and if the site where the body was found was the scene where death occurred.

Did death occur elsewhere? If so, what method of transportation was used to place the body at the scene?

Consider the possibility that if death occurred elsewhere, the body may have been stored at a place where the environmental conditions differ from where the body was found.

Are there multiple scenes, if so, how many?

SCENE PROCEDURES

Polaroids

1. Take Polaroids of all victims as soon as possible.
2. May be used for identification purposes.
3. Take to autopsy.

35mm Stills

1. Photographs are court admissible.
2. Object photographed must be pertinent.
3. The photograph must not be inflammatory.
4. Photograph must be free of distortion and misrepresentation.
5. Photographer must be able to testify to the validity of the photo.
6. Photographs will help maintain proper chain of custody.

Video

1. Video should be taken at every scene, may be more than one.
2. Video should not be used as a substitute for 35 mm stills.
3. Videotape approach, interior, path of flight and body.
4. Video should be narrated.

Notes

1. Useful in preparing a well-written report.
2. Notes made during an investigation can be called into court.
3. Notes are used for recalling places, events, incidents and other pertinent facts of the investigation.
4. Print all notes in permanent black ink.
5. Short phrases should be used, no shorthand or single words.
6. When recording information from witnesses always include full name, date of birth, current address, telephone and workplace information if applicable.
7. Notes should include your observations and pertinent information.

Sketches

1. Photographs and video do not always give the viewer exact distance and sizes of object or true relationship.
2. Provide measurements of size and distance.
3. Depict objects of value and exclude unnecessary detail.
4. Minimum information required:
   a. Title
   b. Case number
   c. Exact location
   d. Time and date of sketch
   e. Scale of sketch "Not To Scale"
   f. Name, ID of badge number of sketch maker
   g. The direction "North"
   h. Measurements within the sketch
   i. The legend

Chapter 19

USE OF BLOOD EVIDENCE

DNA

FOR MANY YEARS SCIENTISTS were limited to determining human blood from animal blood and developing methods for detection of blood. Today we can positively identify individuals such as perpetrators of crime through the use of DNA. DNA fingerprinting is a technique that detects and identifies the location of unique structure with chromosomes. These structures, referred to as enzyme sites, are made of a particular sequence of nucleotides. It is these nucleotides and their sequence that makes each individual so unique and different from everyone else. The only time this is not absolute is in the case of identical twins.

Bodily fluids left at the crime scene can be used as evidence and as a source for DNA. The DNA evidence can be compared with the suspect's blood sample. DNA technology is very important as an investigative tool. This type of evidence can link a suspect or even a victim to a murder scene.

BLOOD SPATTER INTERPRETATION

Violent deaths can produce bloodshed. When blood is acted upon by a physical force, patterns of different sizes and shapes will be deposited on various items at the scene, on clothing on the victim, or in some instances on the suspect. Interpretation of bloodstain patterns can tremendously assist the death investigator.

Valuable data can be detected through an analysis of bloodspatter patterns. Depending on the nature and quantity of bloodstains present, it is possible to reveal the location and position of both the victim and the suspect, the movements of those persons, a possible weapon, as well as the number of actions that caused the bleeding, such as blows or shots. Other facts that may additionally be provided by examination of bloodstain patterns include origin of the bloodstains, direction or type of impact-producing spatter and identification of objects that produce particular patterns.

Bloodspatter interpretation is a science that should be developed and understood by anyone involved with death investigation. Any science that will assist the death investigator in determining the sequence of events leading to the death of an individual should be utilized and understood completely. Interpretation of bloodstains will support or contradict statements and laboratory and pathology findings.

Unfortunately, many law enforcement agencies across the country do not have personnel trained in this field. Bloodspatter interpretation can and will help prove cause and manner of death. It can and has made the difference between a homicide and a suicide. Perhaps police agencies simply are not aware of the value of crime scene reconstruction through the use of bloodspatter interpretation.

Dating back to the late 1800s, there was some mention of bloodspatter analysis having evidentiary value. In 1893, research was being conducted in Austria studying the flight characteristics of blood. In 1904, bloodstain experiments were being conducted in France. Much material was written in 1924 on the thoughts that a perpetrator can be totally free of bloodstains, even when circumstance would indicate that he must be heavily covered in blood.

In 1930, written material indicated that the pools of blood, their size, shape, location, and condition should be noted. It was even suggested this should be done not only around the victim, but the entire vicinity, especially in a homicide. Also in 1930, a gentleman by the name of Calvin Goddard made an unusual and perhaps significant statement in regards to an examination of large pools of blood on a concrete floor at 2122 North Clark Street in Chicago, Illinois. Mr. Goddard indicated that the floor was smooth and flat, but not level. He also noted that blood ran from the head of three of the five victims in parallel streams away from the wall they faced. Goddard went on in his evaluation and eluded that as to the motive for the mass murder, "It was commonly conceded that the Bugs Moran gang had rivals who would find business better if competition were less keen. A dead competitor sells no beer." Mr. Goddard was writing about the St. Valentine's Day Massacre.

Figure 19.1. St. Valentines Day massacre. Note the pools of blood on the floor as described by Calvin Goddard.

The death scene investigation and reconstruction by the use of bloodstain patterns is a tedious time-consuming task. However, the information that can be learned by this type of reconstruction is invaluable. Using bloodstain patterns for reconstruction purposes can recreate the scene and the actions that occurred in the scene. No other investigative tool can currently provide the same results.

The human body has eleven pints of blood. Each pint contains approximately ten thousand dime-size drops of blood. That equates to about 110,000 drops of blood that bloodshedding can produce. Where death investigations are concerned there can be a great wealth of information gained by a detailed study of bloodspatters. It is important to study the size and the shapes of bloodstains. By interpreting bloodspatters it is possible to reconstruct the actual events that caused the bloodstains. All too often the study of bloodspatters has been neglected.

Bloodspatter follows the laws of physical science, it falls with gravity. Free-falling blood falls at about 25 feet per second. A blood drop is like a round sphere or ball. This sphere has surface tension that holds the drop together. The blood drop, held together by surface tension, will not break up in its flight. It is not until the surface tension is broken that the sphere will break up. When the drop strikes a surface such as a wall or floor, the surface tension is broken. The result is bloodspatter.

As to the size of a bloodspatter, obviously the amount of blood will depend on the type of injury. A normal drop of blood is about five-eighths inches in diameter to three-fourths inch in diameter. A drop of blood can also give an indication as to how far the drop fell. Once the volume of a blood drop reaches terminal velocity (25'/sec.), the drop will not increase in size. The drop will reach terminal velocity between five to six feet. Impacted blood from something like a gunshot or airplane propeller will increase terminal velocity. This type of impacted blood is referred to as mist and never travels more that three to four feet from where it was impacted. Distance is dependent upon weight or the volume of the blood drop.

Two Rules

There are two basic rules that apply to the shape of bloodstains:
1. When a drop of blood strikes a surface, perpendicular to its line of flight a circular stain will result. The rounder the stain, the line of flight was perpendicular at impact.
2. When a drop of blood strikes a surface, which is at an angle to its line of flight, an elongated stain will result. The longer the stain, the line of flight was at an angle at impact.

An important aspect of scene reconstruction in bloodspatter is that of measurements. The lengths and widths of selected bloodstains must be measured. Basically, by measuring the width of a stain and dividing that number by the width of the same stain, it will determine the angle that the spatter impacted a surface or object. This impact angle during the reconstruction process can be projected back to where the blood originated.

As a large percentage of deaths are caused by gunshot or stabbing, a significant amount of bloodstains may be present to reconstruct the events that brought about the death. A person trained in bloodspatter interpretation will be able to study the size and shape of spatter, take measurements, and project where the point of origin of the blood-stains. Most likely, additional information from investigating the scene will aid the bloodspatter reconstruction expert.

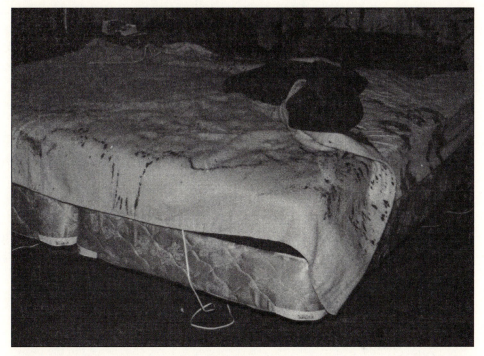

Figure 19.2. Homicide scene where bloodspatter interpretation was used to determine the events that occurred in the bedroom. Apparent trails of blood can be seen from the bed to the floor, and around the end of the bed.

Areas that should be checked for bloodspatter might be the hands or arms, on the weapon, the floor, the walls, the ceiling, and the clothing. Bloodspatter has been found on both the victim and on suspects. Blood on the hands of a suicide victim might be possible. Blood might also be found on the hands of the suspect. Examine everything carefully.

Blood can originate from the victim or the suspect. Through the use of bloodspatter interpretation it is possible to detect the motion of the suspect's direction of flight. The disruptive edge of the spatter will give an indication of direction of travel. It is also achievable that we can determine from the blood drops left by the suspect, from what area of the body the suspect is bleeding by reconstructing the height from which the blood drop fell.

There are several things that the bloodspatter analysts must consider when reconstructing the death scene. The number, location, size and shape of the bloodstains and the type of surface where the blood was deposited. The bloodspatter analysts can then make a selection of bloodstains and by measuring each one, the angle of impact can be calculated. With the use of string lines, a point of convergence can be determined, where bloodshedding occurred. The scene can then be reconstructed, even if the victim is not present in the crime scene.

The bloodspatter reconstructionist can also make a determination of where bleeding occurred on a victim, and where he or she was located at the time of being shot, stabbed or beaten. It is also possible to tell how many times the victim was shot, stabbed, or beaten. It may even be possible to establish where the suspect was standing in relationship to the victim. If the perpetrator was also bleeding, some idea of the location, and what direction he or she traveled can also be established. There is also an opportunity to determine how long ago the bleeding was produced. By studying the drying time of blood as it congeals, this time can be projected as to when bleeding first occurred.

Case History 1

In April of 1984, a female victim was suspected to have shot herself in the head with a small caliber handgun. Bloodspatter evidence at the scene did not match the statements provided by her boyfriend, the only other person in the house at the time of the shooting. Reconstruction of the scene indicated that the girl was on the telephone attempting to make a phone call. Additional information learned from the reconstruction indicated that the victim was moved away from where the telephone was located. The boyfriend received 25 years for murder.

Case History 2

A lady of the evening was found dead in a field in June of 1986. Her head and skull had been crushed in by several blows from a large cement block. She had been struck approximately eight times. The force of the cement block drove her skull into the ground more than seven inches deep. One suspect provided information that while he was present during the murder, he only watched as his accomplice dropped the block on the girl's head eight or nine times. He maintained his innocence during questioning. However, when confronted with the bloodspatter evidence found on his blue jeans, he confessed to have been sitting on the girls chest holding her down, while the block was dropped again and again. The blue jeans showed areas from the knee to the waist impacted with blood.

Case History 3

In the spring of 1988, the prosecutor's office was preparing to go to trial on a case where the victim was badly burned due to having hot grease thrown on her. The female victim was permanently disfigured from the incident. The defense attorney had indicated that the defense was based on the following: The skillet filled with hot grease was sitting on the stove and the defendant accidentally hit the handle of the skillet causing the skillet to be knocked off the stove. When the skillet came off the stove, the grease splashed on the victim's face. I was asked to examine the photographs of the grease stains on the wall. The pictures taken at the time indicated from the directionality of the grease spots the grease was thrown in an upwards motion towards where the victim was standing. The same principles of bloodspatter interpretation were used. The grease was not knocked off the stove as stated by the defendant. The evidence proved that the grease had been thrown. The defendant negotiated a guilty plea when confronted with this information.

Bloodspatter Interpretation

1. Point of origin of blood.
2. Type and direction of impact that produced bloodshedding.
3. Movement and direction of person(s) or object(s).
4. The number of shots or the minimum number of blows.
5. Position of victim and suspect at the time bloodshedding occurred.
6. The distance between the target and the point of origin.

Bloodspatter Characteristics

1. Measure selected number of bloodstains.
2. The location of the bloodstains.
3. The size and the shape of selected bloodstains.
4. The target surface.

Calculation of Impact Angle

1. Measure the width and length of selected bloodstains.
2. Divide the length by the width.
3. Using the sine function, determine the angle the bloodstain impacted the target.

Velocity of Impacted Blood

1. Low velocity or low impact will produce larger drops of blood.
2. Medium velocity occurs when blood is impacted by a force of 5 to 25 ft. per sec. Medium velocity impact will be caused by items such as hammer, bat, or golf club.
3. High velocity occurs greater than 25 ft. per sec. The drops that resemble mist can be caused by gunshot or airplane propellers.

Chapter 20

USE OF HYPNOSIS

EARLIER IN THIS HANDBOOK it was mentioned that the police death investigator should seek out every avenue possible to assist in the investigation. One particular technique available to support the death investigator is the use of investigative and forensic hypnosis. Everyone is somewhat familiar with hypnosis, although it is often misunderstood. When most people think of hypnosis, they immediately think of something like a stage hypnotist. A stage hypnotist is an entertainer that, through the use of hypnosis, gets people to do and say silly things. Obviously, with this kind of impression of hypnosis, it is not often thought of as an investigative tool.

The use of hypnosis actually dates back before the birth of Christ. It was used in religion and healing. Hypnosis is often thought of as mind control and, therefore, many people have a fear of being hypnotized. It was not until the 1950s that the use of hypnosis was approved by various medical and psychological associations.

A definition of hypnosis is a state of deep relaxation with an altered state of consciousness. The word hypnosis is derived from the Greek word hypnos, which means to sleep. It is important to note that all hypnosis is self hypnosis. A person actually hypnotizes himself or herself; the hypnotist merely guides a person into hypnosis by suggestion. Hypnosis occurs when relaxation of the conscious mind promotes concentration and suggestibility to suggestion.

This means a person is hypnotized when they are totally relaxed and able to concentrate greatly. When hypnotized, a person reaches a state of heightened relaxation and awareness. During the hypnotic state, the subject can often remember past events that they normally could not recall. The person can concentrate on specific past events to vividly and accurately recall many details.

Scientific research has revealed that our brain retains everything that we see and hear. Most information we perceive is not needed to function and, therefore, is stored away in the subconscious level of the brain. When a person is hypnotized, the mind is completely relaxed, facilitating the retrieval of information otherwise lost to the conscious mind.

My explanation for this retaining of stored memory is that our mind works like a dual recording system. As information is absorbed into the brain it goes into the conscious memory also associated with short-term memory. The information moves through the conscious to the subconscious or from short-term to long-term memory. As stated earlier; hypnosis is an altered state of consciousness. When hypnotized, the subconscious or long-term memory can recall information.

The use of hypnosis in criminal investigations began in the late 1950s. By the mid-1970s a widespread interest in investigative hypnosis had developed. Quite simply, hypnosis used in criminal investigations as a tool to obtain or develop new investigative leads, can enhance or refresh the memory of a witness or victim.

A defense attorney may suggest that the suspect undergo hypnosis to get at the truth of the investigation. The defendant's attorney may also suggest his client undergo hypnosis to determine the suspect's state of mind before or during the commission of a crime. However, hypnosis should not be used to elicit information from a suspect. The suspect could fake hypnosis or the suspect could lie under hypnosis. Lastly, the defense attorney may object to any courtroom presentation or any information obtained from the defendant through the use of hypnosis. Hypnosis should never be used as a shortcut through an investigation. The prosecutor should be consulted before using hypnosis during an investigation. The laws pertaining to the use of hypnosis varies from state to state. Information obtained might not be admissible if the current jurisdictional laws relating to the use of hypnosis are not followed closely.

How the witness or victim is approached when asked to undergo hypnosis may adversely affect the value or success of a hypnotic interview. It is important to know what to say and how to say it when attempting to set up an interview. You can best achieve this permission from your witness or victim by knowing a little about how the hypnotic interview will be conducted. The subject that you would like to have hypnotized should be informed that a competent hypnotist will be doing the hypnosis. Explain the reasons you want them to be hypnotized, that you know they want to help, and the harder a person tries to remember something, the harder it is to recall. Finally, assure them that they will not do anything or say anything that they do not want to; no dark secrets are going to be revealed.

The actual investigative interview is broken down into three equally important interviews. The first is what is called the preinduction interview before hypnosis. The second part is the hypnotic interview conducted while the subject is under hypnosis. The third is the postinduction interview that is conducted after the subject is brought out of hypnosis. People have recalled pertinent information while in the preinduction interview, simply because they started to relax.

Preinduction Interview

During the preinduction interview, the hypnotist meets the subject to be hypnotized for the first time. At this point and until the subject and the hypnotist leave, the interview, the conversation, and interview is video recorded. The subject is then asked a series of questions pertaining to any prior hypnotic experience. What is the subject's conception of hypnosis, the subject's mental and physical condition and whether or not the subject is under any doctor's care or on any medication is discussed The hypnotic interview process is explained and the subject is advised about the use of recording equipment.

The hypnotist will also give several assurances at this time affirming that only the crime under investigation will be discussed, that the person will be very much aware of what is being said and done, that the person will retain complete self control during the interview, and will only remember as much as is comfortable for them to remember. The subject will also be assured that no personal questions will be asked and that nothing embarrassing will be allowed to happen. The person will be able to hear other sounds around. Most investigative or forensic hypnotists have a consent form. At this time the subject will be asked to read and sign the consent form.

Induction

At this point the hypnotic interview begins or is accomplished by one or more induction methods available to the hypnotist. The object of the induction is to induce hypnosis or to produce a state of deep relaxation. Once the person is in hypnosis, the hypnotist may use other techniques to deepen the subject's state of relaxation. This often aids the subject with memory refreshment.

This deepening is usually done through the use of imagery or fantasy. By asking the subject to imagine those things that are relaxing to them, their state of relaxation will deepen. This relaxation can be taken too deeply, then it is difficult for the subject to verbally communicate. Once the hypnotist feels that the subject is at the right depth of hypnosis, the subject is then regressed in time to the time frame in question. This can be accomplished again through the use of imagery, a clock or a calendar that goes backwards can often be imagined by the subject.

The hypnotist then allows the subject to recall the events that occurred during that questioned time period. The hypnotist must use extreme caution to avoid the possibility of making any suggestion of facts to the subject being hypnotized. The forensic hypnotist will go through the hypnotic interview in three steps. First, the hypnotist will allow the subject to feebly recall information as they can. Next, the hypnotist will guide the subject to recall more pertinent information from the information gained in free recall. Lastly, the hypnotist will use direct recall to ascertain specific facts about previously recalled information during the hypnotic session.

Postinduction Interview

Once the hypnotist has obtained the information or can go no further with the hypnotic session, the subject is brought out of the hypnotic state for the postinduction interview. This is a debriefing period where the hypnotist and the hypnotized person discuss what the subject could recall after being in hypnosis. This interview also allows the person to recall this information again, while not under hypnosis.

This time permits the subject the opportunity to fully awaken or return to an alert state, before being allowed to leave. At the point where a subject comes out of hypnosis, he or she is quite susceptible to go under again quite rapidly. It is at the conclusion of this interview that the recording processed is stopped. These hypnotic interviews can last from two to six hours in length.

Once the hypnotic interview has concluded, any information that was obtained will be turned over to the investigating agency. Any information gathered from a hypnotic interview must be checked and substantiated. The information collected may be true, partly true, or totally wrong. Keep in mind that although the information may not be accurate, the witness may not be deliberately attempting to mislead the police. What information the subject recalled is the way they recall it. Sometimes the subject will have gaps in their memory. The subject may confabulate, or fill in the gaps of their memory, with information that might not be correct. Again, this confabulation is not an attempt to deceive the police or complicate the investigation.

SUMMARY

Hypnosis when properly used can be a valuable investigative tool. When in a hypnotic state, the subject experiences a high level of relaxation and awareness during which affected memory-retrieved techniques can be utilized by the hypnotist. Hypnosis should be used only after all investigative leads have been exhausted. The objective of hypnosis is to supplement other investigative efforts. Any information obtained from the hypnotic session must be verified. The failure to utilize investigative hypnosis properly will lead to court decisions opposing the use of this precious investigative instrument. Once this happens, law enforcement loses.

Case History 1

A neighboring county sheriff's office requested that I do a hypnotic interview with a subject that had been interviewed as a witness to a burglary more than a year old. It had also been more than a year since the subject had been interviewed; however, the sheriff's detective was sure that the witness had seen something. The subject had driven by the isolated area of the daytime burglary. Within minutes of being placed under hypnosis, the subject revealed a description of the car used by the burglars. During the guided phase of the interview while under hypnosis, the subject provided the license plate to the vehicle. The sheriff's detective checked the plate and found that it was registered to a car like the hypnotized subject had provided. The detective contacted and interviewed the car's owner and was given a confession to the burglary.

Case History 2

At the request of a city police sex crimes detective I conducted a hypnotic interview with the female victim of a sexual assault. The victim emphatically claimed that the suspect crept up behind her, forced her into a bathroom of a laundromat and closed the door without her ever getting an opportunity to see his face. During the hypnotic interview, the subject was taken to a point in her refreshed memory where she was able to see his face. The city police detective, during the hypnotic interview, made a composite of the suspect that was later disseminated to all police agencies. Within one day the suspect was identified, picked out of a line up, and subsequently convicted of a felony. All from the testimony of a victim who could not recall seeing the suspect.

Case History 3

Not all hypnotic interviews are as successful. If any information can be developed that was not previously known, then the session was somewhat successful. I was asked by a city police homicide detective to do a hypnotic interview with a survivor of a brutal ax attack where three other people were murdered. The subject was placed into a state of hypnosis; however, very little information was brought out. The subject, who had suffered some pertinent brain injury as a result of the being struck with the ax, simply had repressed his memory and did not want to recall the events that took place that day.

Chapter 21

USE OF PSYCHICS

MANY YEARS AGO WHEN I first started investigating deaths, I read a book about homicide investigation. In one area of the book the author talked about the use of psychics. In a heading that categorized clairvoyants, fortune tellers and mediums, the author relates that he, "Knows of no case where any valuable information was obtained by such methods." The author went on to say, "It would be wonderful indeed if it were possible to solve a homicide by contacting the departed spirit and him disclose the facts in the case." The author continued stating, "The amazing thing is that even today police officers often try to derive information from such sources. Such a consultation generally indicates an attempt to repair damage caused by an inadequate investigation at the time the body was found." The author was in the medical field.

Although psychics may not be for everybody, I know death investigators across the country that have in the past taken advantage of information provided by a psychic and will continue to do so in the future. Many of the police officers that I worked with were skeptics. I have always tried to maintain that the police death investigator should keep an open mind during any investigation. Towards the end of my teaching career, I made "Dealing with Psychics" part of the curriculum of my death investigation classes.

In the more than 20 years spent investigating deaths, I have come in contact with a great number of psychics. In dealing with some, I would certainly agree with the author that stated nothing valuable was ever ascertained. However, there are some psychics that, for some unexplained reason, are able to provide pertinent information or facts about a specific case. Admittedly the accurate clairvoyants are few and far between. It only takes one good one to make any death investigator a believer. Psychics that are able to provide information seem to hit on about 40 percent accuracy. However, some psychics have been able to provide information that is correct 60 percent of the time.

The use of a psychic must not be done as a shortcut through an investigation. However, there comes a time, in some cases that no new or additional information can be developed. A psychic may be able to provide some minute fact that can restart an otherwise stagnate investigation. Expert psychic testimony is not accepted in any court, therefore, any information that a psychic provides must be checked and corroborated.

Any psychic that I have ever dealt with has not attempted to contact the victim to obtain the facts of the case. Some psychics may want to touch or hold an object that belonged to the victim, but that is the only contact with the victim. Most psychics will say they do not actually talk with anyone, but are shown things that represent the past. A few psychics have indicated that angels reveal visions of past events.

Different psychics work in different ways. Some will just start talking about what they see or are being shown. Other psychics will provide one answer to one question. In some instances, the psychic will ask basic questions that focus on the facts of the case. Some psychics will want to go to the scene, while others prefer to work over the telephone.

Psychics may tell you that they use a combination of skills such as clairvoyance to see the events and clairaudience to hear the events. A medium is considered to have the ability to communicate with those individuals that may have gone to the other side.It is interesting to hear that some psychics say they knew they were clairvoyant at an early age. Others state it was not until they were much older that they developed their abilities. Several psychics have said the natural ability to be a clairvoyant is in everyone, but not everyone has the knowledge to fully develop the gift. I have also heard of people that were struck by lightning or had some type of near-death experience and then exhibited clairvoyant abilities.

I have felt comfortable with only two of the psychics that I personally have ever worked with. A psychic I will call "G," was involved in two different homicides. During the first meeting I was not present. A police officer had been murdered while on patrol in a rural isolated area. I was the first officer to approach the slain officer. I called his name, then realizing he was dead I returned to the squad car to request assistance. Over a period of time it was felt that a stolen vehicle that was recovered was involved.

The psychic G said the stolen car had been used in the murder of the police officer. G also told us that for some reason when she was near the car she wanted to go to Pawnee. Pawnee was a small community several miles away. G was able to tell us everything that was inside the vehicle. G also said that the officer stayed above his body for some time after he was killed. The officer could not believe he was dead. The psychic says she hears the name Terry, my name, being called. I always believed that when I called the officers name, he might have called mine. G also said we would solve the case but it would take many years.

It was not until after the arrest of the murderer 17 years later did all the pieces fit. The man charged and convicted of the murder of the police officer had in fact stolen the car; the car was stolen to go to Pawnee to rob the bank.

In this case, a 40 percent of the information provided was accurate. Even with this information, new information or leads were developed. In a different homicide case G was unable to provide anything of value about the murder, the victim or the suspect. It was interesting to note that as this psychic rose in notoriety, the ability seemed to decrease.

At this point one might question the value in using psychics. Judging from these two cases, it would be understandable why one would consider involving a psychic. If this were the case, a whole chapter would not have been set aside to discuss the use of psychics.

When I first met this next psychic, she arrived at my office with an attorney. The attorney, whom I had known and respected for several years, indicated the lady with him was a psychic. The attorney proceeded to ask if we wanted her help it was fine, and if we did not, this was fine, too. If we did not want to talk with her, they would leave.

I did not have much success with psychics in the past, but one has to keep an open mind. We had just started working on an abduction of an 18-year-old girl. Her car had been found late at night in the middle of the country. We had very few leads in the case until the body was found in a cornfield exactly one week later and at this point we knew the victim had been stabbed.

The psychic, whom I shall call "DT," said the girl had been killed the same night she was abducted and dumped where she was found.

DT went on to say several men and perhaps a woman was also involved in the murder. DT said the people waited for the girl to come by and then they grabbed and killed her. DT went on to say that out of all the people involved one stuck out as being very mean. DT told us she saw the name "TOM" on the back of a belt and Tom had cold black eyes.

When suspects were finally developed, we learned four men and a woman waited in the country for someone to come along. The men planned to flag down a car and rob the first person that came along. The missing girl was their victim. She was taken from her car and stabbed immediately. They placed her in another car and drove her to where her body was found. During the interviews all the participants indicated that Tom was the instigator. Tom had cold, black eyes.

This case alone was enough to convince me to always keep an open mind when it comes to psychics. But my investigative relationship with DT was about to take my belief to a new level. We had received a missing persons report about an individual named Harvey who worked at a gas station. He had not been seen or heard from for about a month. A couple of detectives, almost in a joking manner, said why don't you call your psychic friend. They went on to say no one knew where Harvey was and information had not been been released about the disappearance to the media or public.

I did call DT. After telling DT it was "me," she asked if I was calling about Harvey. In great shock of what I just heard, I told her I was in fact calling about Harvey. DT informed me after Harvey got off work from a gas station, he had been taken out, murdered, and then transported to another location. My mind could not accept what I was hearing. The psychic was actually waiting for me to call and she had started her psychic investigation before I placed the call. Lastly, DT was able to direct us fifty miles to where Harvey's body was buried. We were not able to find the body from the psychics directions, but did find Harvey less than a mile away. DT said that if we could fly over the area, I would see a large tree, larger than any other. The body would be within a mile to the left of the tree. The body was found within a mile to the right of the large tree. We subsequently arrested a husband and wife for the murder of Harvey.

I truly enjoyed working with DT who always attributed success to help from the angels and the work that they did. According to DT, we all have angels that are with us. My angel is a female. Working with

DT was normally in person; however, DT could be just as accurate over the telephone. I would ask DT questions I wanted to know. DT would write on a notebook what she was shown by the angels. At the end of our time together, DT would give the notebook to me. DT's involvement was finished and it was up to me to do whatever with the information.

To reiterate, psychics may not be for everybody. It is the decision of each death investigator as to whether or not they want to utilize the services of a psychic in his or her death investigations. I can only suggest that you keep an open mind. When conducting a death investigation and nothing seems to be going right, help might just be a telephone call away.

Chapter 22

STUDIES AND EXPERIMENTS

A S YOU HAVE READ THROUGHOUT THIS HANDBOOK, I have mentioned several studies and experiments that were related to the investigation of death which have been conducted for more than 20 years. The purpose for conducting these studies and experiments was to collect information that would be of assistance, not only to me, but to others involved in death investigation. These studies and experiments provided valuable data on specific topics. It is easier to understand what you observe at a death scene if you know what you are looking for and what you expect to find. The same holds true for death-related studies and experiments that will help you understand why or how a death occurs.

During my career as a police death investigator I conducted studies related to deaths, cocaine excited delirium-related deaths, homicide cases, and several gunshot tests for the purpose of range determination and the presence of unburned gun powder. I also performed experiments with maggots, and the characteristics of blood in flight. Each of these studies and experiments were conducted with the idea that precious knowledge could be gained. This knowledge was a definite benefit, as it allowed me the opportunity to have the findings of the research and to compare those findings with a particular form of death. I was able to see the results of the experiments and compare those results with observations made at a crime scene. These experiments also provided an indication of how certain things originated at the scene.

Now that we have entered the computer age, it is quite easy to document information gathered from a study or experiment. There are a great number of computer software programs available that allow you to create your own database. These software programs help you to manage the database by allowing you to do things, such as: create a format or fields for data to be entered, add and update data, run a pre-designed report, perform calculations, prepare graphs and charts and many more functions. A search of any computer store will reveal an infinite number of inexpensive programs that will perform any operation that you will need. It is not necessary to invest a lot of money as the prices for computers are quite reasonable. Some people feel their current computer system is too old or outdated to create databases. The system I use for storing the databases that I have has an 85 megabyte hard-drive and has 20 megahertz of speed. I run 18 separate programs from the disk operating system.

You, as a death investigator, or as one who is interested in the investigation of death, might want to seriously consider conducting your own studies or experiments. The studies or experiments that I conducted may interest you to create your own research. You may have thought of other studies or experiments that would be of interest or benefit to you in your law enforcement career. Any information that will be helpful is worth your effort. Conducting studies and experiments are educational and can be a lot of fun. Because of my background in bloodspatter interpretation and my association and membership with the International Association of Bloodstain Pattern Analysts, I have performed most of my experiments with the use of blood. Those experiments include the following: dropping blood from different heights and impact angles, impacting a volume of blood with various forces; including gunshots, and experiments with the movement or blood in motion. I hope in the near future, to do some experiments with blood and the effect of fire.

Experiments with maggots are also educational and fun. It is fascinating to watch the maggots as they conduct their feeding frenzy. These experiments can be set up on a hot, dry, and humid summer day with just a piece of rotting meat. You can see them as they feed, how fast they feed and you can even feel the heat they produce. You can make up your own maggot experiment, carefully observing the blowfly and maggot activity, taking very copious notes. The next time you are sent to a death case on a hot summer day, you will look at the maggot a lot differently.

Figure 22.1. Testing of various types of gunshots fired into blood. The tests were conducted at the Department of Pathology, Memorial Medical Center, Springfield, Illinois.

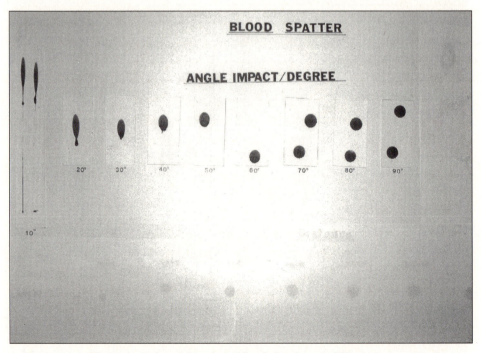

Figure 22.2. The test results of dropping blood droplets at different impact angles.

GLOSSARY

Abrasion: Tearing away layers of epidermis.

Accident: An unexpected, undesirable event.

Adipocere: A condition in which tissues become soaplike.

Age Progression: Advancing the subject's age in the hypnotic trance.

Age Regression: Lowering the subject's age in the hypnotic trance.

Amnesia: The loss of memory.

Angle of Impact: The angle at which blood strikes a target surface.

Anxiety: Painful uneasiness of mind.

Back Spatter: Blood which is directed back towards the force that caused the spatter.

Ballistics: Projectile in motion, after it leaves the barrel of a firearm.

Bore: The inside of a barrel.

Bullet: A non-spherical projectile for use in a rifled barrel.

Cast-off Spatter: Blood which is cast or flung from a moving object due to change in direction or speed.

Confabulation: Filling in memory gaps with distorted information.

Conscious: State of being aware of an inward state.

Contact Spatter: The result of a bloody object coming in contact with a non-bloody object.

Contusion: A bruise due to subsurface hemorrhage.

Coroner: An officer responsible for deciding cause and manner of death.

Corpse: A deceased human body.

Cut: A wound where length is greater than depth.

Death: The loss of life, failure of respiratory, cardiovascular and nervous system.

Decomposition: Postmortem decaying of the body.

Environment: The circumstances or conditions that surround one.

Fetishism: Having a sexual interest in a specific object, item or thing.

153

Firearm: An assembly of a barrel and action from which a projectile is propelled by products of combustion.

Forensic: Used in legal proceedings, from a legal aspect.

    Anthropology: Science that studies the physical characteristic of humans.

    Entomology: The study of insects and other arthropods.

    Pathology: A study of the nature of disease.

    Toxicology: The study of poisons.

Forward Spatter: Blood which is directed in the same direction as the force that caused the spatter.

Fraticide: One that murders his own brother or sister.

Fracture: A break of any bone.

Genocide: The deliberate and systematic killing of a racial, political or cultural group.

Gauge: The number of lead balls of bore diameter that equal one pound. Thus, a 12 gauge is the diameter of a round ball (lead) 1/12th of a pound.

Hematoma: Accumulation of blood in tissues, due to internal hemorrhage.

Homicide: The crime of unlawfully killing someone.

Hyperthermia: Abnormally high body temperature.

Hyperventilation: Rapid or deep respiration resulting in abnormal low levels of carbon dioxide in the blood.

Hypothermia: Abnormally low body temperature.

Hypoxia: A deficiency of oxygen.

Infanticide: Murder of an infant soon after birth.

Masochism: Attaining sexual pleasure from receiving pain.

Matricide: Murder of a mother by her son or daughter.

Methodology: A body of practices, procedures and rules used in a specialty.

Murderous: Having the purpose or capability of murder.

Patricide: Murder of a father by his son or daughter.

Phenomenon: An exceptional, unusual, or abnormal thing or occurrence.

Phobia: An unreasonable fear.

Pistol: A handgun in which the chamber is part of the barrel.

Rifle: A firearm having a rifling in the bore and designed to be fired from the shoulder.

Rigor Mortis: The postmortem affect of progressive rigidity of the body due to the accumulation of lactic acid in the dying muscles.

Sadism: Attaining sexual pleasure from acts of cruelty or infliction of pain.

Secondary Spatter: Blood drops that originate from a blood volume when the blood volume strikes a surface.

Shotgun: A smooth bore shoulder arm designed to fire shotshells.

Skeptic: One who doubts or disbelieves.

Stab: Wound penetration is deeper than the width.

Stippling: Small hemorrhage marks on the skin produced by the impact of gunpowder particles.

Suicide: Deliberately killing one's self.

Suggestion: An idea which is offered to the subject for acceptance.

Systematic: An organized method or procedure.

Target: The surface on which blood is deposited.

Transfer Patterns: When a bloody object leaves an identifiable pattern on a non-bloody object.

Transvestism: One who prefers an opposite sexual role such as cross dressing.

Trauma: Injury, shock of the resulting condition.

Viscera: The larger, interior organs in the lower part of the body.

Wad: In shotshells, may be between the propellant and shot, or over top of the shot held in place with a rolled crimp, or may be a plastic sleeve which holds the shot.

INDEX